METAPHYSICAL WARRIOR

BOOKS BY JEF7REY HILDNER (aka ELIOT PLUM and HENRY TRUCKS) **:**

AUTHOR, BOOK DESIGNER, AND PUBLISHER
METAPHYSICAL WARRIOR: Meditations on the art & science of life
DAEDALUS 9 | THE ARCHITECT PAINTER [improv 1.0]
HENRY TRUCKS—Painter : ancient myths meet modern landscapes | 1995-2010
MISFITZ BECAUSE: What Doesn't Belong—and Why? Mind-Teasers!
GARCHES 1234: Remembering the Mathematics of the Ideal Villa—
            An Essay on Le Corbusier's 1927 Villa de Monzie/Stein
PICASSO LESSONS: The Sixth Woman of Les Demoiselles d'Avignon

CONTRIBUTOR
REMEMBRANCE AND THE DESIGN OF PLACE by Frances Downing
ARCHITECTURAL FORMALISM by Anay Hakan—with Peggy Deamer, Rosalind Krauss,
            Robert Slutzky and Colin Rowe

METAPHYSICAL WARRIOR
Meditations on the art & science of life

JEF7REY HILDNER

Σ

METAPHYSICAL WARRIOR: Meditations on the art & science of life
Copyright © 2014 by JEF7REY HILDNER
FIRST EDITION

ISBN-13: 9780692348116 Paperback | Color [CreateSpace]
ISBN-13: 9781300440994 Paperback | Color [Lulu]
ISBN-13: 9781300441014 Paperback | B&W [Lulu]
ISBN-13: 9780974492223 Hardcover | Color [Blurb (TAPP ISBN)]

All rights reserved.
No part of this book may be reproduced in any form or by any electronic or mechanical means (including information storage and retrieval systems) without written permission from
THE ARCHITECT PAINTER PRESS.

Published by
THE ARCHITECT PAINTER PRESS
SACRAMENTO 95818
www.thearchitectpainterpress.com

BOOK CREATED, DESIGNED, AND PRODUCED BY JEF7REY HILDNER.
Unless noted otherwise, the author created all photographs, illustrations, and art.

"Free the angel" reprinted with permission from the December 5, 2011 issue of the *Christian Science Sentinel*. © 2011 The Christian Science Publishing Society (sentinel.christianscience.com).

Special thank you to copyeditor Laura Dawn Middleton.
Not that we haven't missed something—let us know: press@thearchitectpainter.com.

∞

life goal: **CONTROL**AND**SOUL**

π

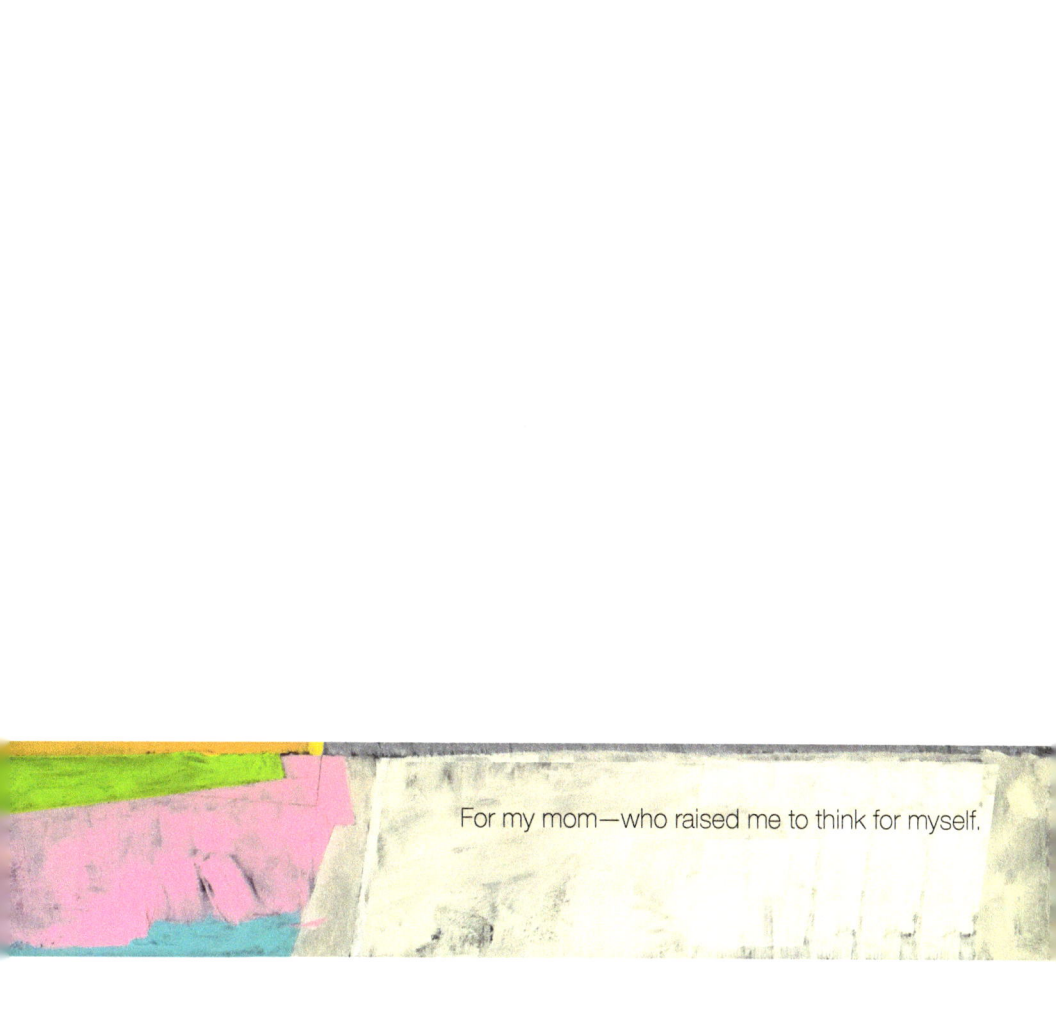

For my mom—who raised me to think for myself.

A writer's prayer

EVERY WORD

MIND writes every word,
Shapes every sentence,
Forms every paragraph,
Builds the piece
Line by line—
Beginning,
Middle,
End.

CONTENTS

PREFACE: Eternity Now — 19

INTRODUCTION: Divinity And Humanity—The Secret Code — 23

PUBLIC | 37

1. Journey Through The Labyrinth — 39
2. Suit Up — 67
3. Illusions — 71
4. Opportunity Will Find You — 77
5. The Scientific Way — 81
6. Flight 1866 — 93
7. Free The Angel — 107
8. Wake-Up Call — 119
9. Dr. Truth — 127

PRIVATE | 137

a. Thought Paint — 139
b. Mentors — 155
c. Frank Bold-Write, Architect — 171
d. Metadata — 179

immortality / longevity / eternity ∞

PREFACE
Eternity Now

You don't have to die. It's not required.
—jazz musician Ornette Coleman

I wrote this book to find out what I think. I fill it with meditations and speculations and offbeat fragments of inspiration that express my worldview and mark my zigzag path through life.

I see this book as a way of giving back: a long thank you note to the many people who have helped me climb the ladder of enlightenment. And I don't want my life's lessons and insights to vanish when I go to Jupiter (my way of saying, kick the bucket). I want what little hard-won wisdom I've picked up along the way to live on and hopefully help other people.

My hope reflects a universal desire, because I believe that we all yearn for our lives to matter.

Call my desire a quest for immortality—or more realistically, a quest for immortality's echo: longevity.

If you look up the word *longevity*, you will find that it not only means "a long duration of individual life; length of life." The word *longevity* also means "permanence, durability," which evokes the meaning of *immortality*.

I keep my dictionary open to the definition of *longevity*. It helps me recall that Job, according to the Bible, lived more than 140 years, and this reminds me to set my sight on the bright star of long life—undiminished—long life that ideally gains in resilience and strength, creativity and productivity, progressively expressing our innate, spiritually-based permanence and durability.

And here's what you find if you look up *durability*: "able to exist for a long time without significant deterioration; designed to be durable—synonyms: see *lasting*."

Click on *lasting* and you discover more about intrinsic qualities of longevity:
—*lasting*: "a capacity to continue indefinitely"
—*permanent*: "designed or planned to stand or continue indefinitely"
—*durable*: "power to resist destructive agencies."

I want my creative work and ideas to continue indefinitely as a catalyst and source of inspiration to others. Even more, *I want to continue indefinitely. I want to resist destructive agencies.* Don't you?

Well, here's the secret of life: We can.

Pierre Teilhard de Chardin, the 20th-century French Jesuit and philosopher said, "We are not human beings having a spiritual experience. We are spiritual beings having a human experience." I think so too. And if we could cut through the fog of misperceptions and misconceptions, as the beam from a lighthouse cuts through the night, we would see clearly this deep truth: *We are designed to last. We have the power to resist destructive agencies. We are permanent, and durable—invincible. Immortal.*

Metaphysical warriors see themselves and others in this ideal way.

Metaphysical warriors know this: As spiritual beings, we have the power to see through mortal illusion, delusion, and confusion, and intelligently navigate the treacherous Labyrinth of human experience. We can trust that lightning bolts of insight, skill, and courage will propel our journey. Shooting stars of intuition, foresight, composure, and compassion will light our path. Darkness cannot defeat us. And no adversary has the power to run out our clock.

**Right now, this moment and forever,
we coexist with and express Life
as sunbeams coexist with and express the sun.**

Yes, we may fall short in this lifetime of fully experiencing this metaphysical ideal. But I believe that we will get a lot of practice as we move through various lifetimes along our grand eternal Cosmic Journey. And we can start practicing now.

JEF7REY HILDNER / SACRAMENTO, CA

"Eternity is not the hereafter.... This is it. If you don't get it here, you won't get it anywhere. The experience of eternity right here and now is the function of life." —Joseph Campbell

The path of safety will open up for you from where you least imagine it.
—Virgil, *The Aeneid*

INTRODUCTION
Divinity And Humanity—The Secret Code

> **We cannot teach people anything; we can only help them discover it within themselves.** —Galileo Galilei

I don't know how much my insights shape other people, but I do know that other people's insights shape me. The spiritual wisdom of others blends naturally with my own epiphanies to create who I am, giving me identity and form, contouring the sheet metal of my being and inspiring an ever-dawning realization of the way the world works, despite the thick fog of false concepts that blinds me to the truth.

The sun doesn't rise or set—the earth spins. Remember that. It could help you, as it has helped me. Because that fact reminds me to cut through illusions and off-base descriptions of reality with the laser light of science. I've got a long way to go to do this consistently and fearlessly, to become a metaphysical master, but I've begun the trip, and I plan to keep going and never turn back.

Were it not for the heroes who have gone before me, I think I would have been roadsided by now, waiting for a tow truck that never comes or wobbling through life on a flat tire I couldn't repair, cursing my misfortune and wondering, *Why? Why is life like this?* I would feel lost, flummoxed, discouraged, resentful, and upset, stumped by why this happens or that doesn't happen and what to do to stay on track.

I owe so much to two special heroes: mythologist Joseph Campbell and the discoverer and founder of Christian Science, Mary Baker Eddy.

MAPS OF THE WORLD

Campbell and Eddy have given me maps of the world. These two people unlocked the secret code of reality. Viewed separately, their discoveries provide only a necessary basis for comprehending life's setup, not a sufficient basis. But viewed together, their complementary revelations paint the big picture. So if you want to travel safely through mortality's maze—equipped with insight, foresight, resilience, valor, and health—then I encourage you to get the scoop (and the heads-up) from both of these explorers.

My view sets me apart from Christian Scientists who feel that Eddy explained in her book *Science and Health with Key to the Scriptures* what we need to know about human existence to cope with trouble and thrive. And I assume that my view could vex ardent Joseph Campbell followers who resist talk of religion and know little about Christian Science.

If you embrace the discoveries of only one of these two people, without knowledge of what the other has figured out, hoping to keep your ship of life afloat and avoid the rocks without the double-beam of these twin lighthouses—well, all I can say is, I tried that. For 47 years, I practiced the teachings of Eddy's Christian Science but without the benefit of Campbell's compatible research, which reveals the coherent, archetypal structure and characters—the deep and practical, abstract essence—of the human storyboard. I didn't know about his discovery of "The Hero's Journey": an inner and outer quest in which a hero departs from her ordinary world, undergoes transformation in a new world, and returns home to share what she has learned, having encountered threshold guardians, enemies, shapeshifters, and allies throughout her triumphant adventure.

Eddy's life exemplified this universal paradigm of the Hero's Journey. But she could not fully know this, because she passed on in 1910, when Campbell was six years old.

LOOPHOLES

I couldn't have made it through those first 47 years of my life, let alone the years that have followed, without Eddy's discovery of the underlying metaphysics of existence, wherein harmony, intelligence, joy—Good in countless forms—constitute the durable substance of our being. I've seen vivid proof that the Life-Science Eddy discovered transforms human life and sets you free. But Eddy left the door ajar. She maintained that the way that life is learned isn't through human edification but through divine revelation and understanding. On the one hand: True—if we take *life* to mean divine life (Life). On the other hand: Not entirely true—if we take *life* to mean also human life. (See sidebar.) Because the way we learn about core aspects of human life—and gain mature capacities, including people skills, wisdom, and grit—springs not only from spiritual understanding, but also from Spirit-inspired human understanding.

Eddy said, "Christian Science teaches only that which is spiritual and divine, and not human" (*Science and Health*, p. 99). Little wonder then that Christian Scientists might undervalue the benefits of learning about the human dimension of experience, because that would logically require turning to a source other than Christian Science—which many earnest Christian Scientists believe that a true adherent of the religion wouldn't do.

And so many earnest Christian Scientists draw from their study of *Science and Health* an odd take on life, which naturally leads to self-deception and self-sabotage. Despite Eddy's assertion that Christian Science *doesn't* teach that which is human, many members of her Church maintain that Christian Science *does* sufficiently equip people to understand what they need to know about their human lives: No one need turn to other sources to develop skill-sets of, say, interpersonal and intrapersonal intelligence, because Christian Science teaches you what you need to know about the art & science of being human, and so if you do look elsewhere for instruction, you look in vain.

I disagree. Don't get me wrong. I still believe that Christian Science reveals the truth about Life: It is spiritual, good, ever-present, and eternal. And my grasp of this metaphysical reality impacts my everyday experience in good and tangible ways.

But I no longer live under the false impression that Christian Science also fully prepares me to navigate astutely and skillfully through human life.

life. A quick aside about two ways that Eddy used the word *life*:

By *life*, Eddy sometimes meant spiritual life—not life that we associate with matter, mortality, or human experience, but rather *true* life, transcendent life, life above the plane of physics. Here's an example: "The Science Jesus taught and lived must triumph over all material beliefs about life, substance, and intelligence, and the multitudinous errors growing from such beliefs" (*Science and Health*, p. 43). When she used *life* in this sense, Eddy meant life undying—life so substantial and real that it transcends all time and can never expire or leave us, for we are the very essence of life! Defined this way, *life* flows continuously through our being (and as our being) as a coexistent expression of capital-letter *Life*, a synonym for God, in much the same way that light flows continuously via sunbeams as coexistent expressions of the Sun.

Eddy saw that looking for the true meaning and substance of life by looking to matter was to look in vain: You can no more discern the true nature of your life and my life—our one Life—by studying matter than you can find the true substance and source of the moon's light by studying the moon.

The source of the moon's (unwaning) light can't be found by examining the moon's surface or by drilling ever-deeper into its core. No. You have to look beyond the moon and undergo a mental shift in perspective. Only then can you discover and benefit from the knowledge that despite appearances the source of the moon's light is the sun. The moon only appears to generate light, which is simply an illusion.

Likewise, as Eddy discovered, we have to look beyond the illusion of mortality and matter, beyond our apparent human form, to see the true, sustaining, non-stop flow motion of life's spiritual and incorporeal reality.

Eddy used the word *life* hundreds of times in *Science and Health*. But she didn't always use the word to refer to our Life-sourced spiritual substance. Sometimes she used the word to refer to our human experience.

Take this example, where Eddy referred to herself: "She closed her College, October 29, 1889, in the height of its prosperity with a deep-lying conviction that the next two years of her life should be given to the preparation of the revision of SCIENCE AND HEALTH, which was published in 1891" (p. xii).

Or this example, where Eddy referred to Jesus and makes a clear distinction: "Through the magnitude of his human life, he demonstrated the divine Life" (p. 54).

I take a different tack from Christian Scientists who feel that people need no other life-reference books than the Bible and *Science and Health*.

Really? No other books can amplify and teach us about life—spiritually-girded human life that the psalmist David embraced when he said, "Surely goodness and mercy shall follow me all the days of my life"? Other than the Bible, no ancient, time-tested, deeply human (yet Mind-inspired) strategies for safety, survival, and well-being can help us? No freshly glimpsed non-Christian Science wisdom-principles can assist us in our everyday lives? No archetypal blueprint can guide us through this human maze and help us meet adversity as its master?

Fortunately, many other worthwhile books have been written by other human representatives of Mind. Or I'd be lost. Because I truly believe that Eddy meant what she said and said what she meant: "Christian Science teaches only that which is spiritual and divine, and not human." And learning about the spiritual and divine while turning a blind eye to the human is like a sailor who navigates by looking to the North Star, but doesn't look at a map of the earth. So I look at a map of the earth to sail the waters of human life. And I filter what I learn through the spiritual perspective of life that I gain from the North Star of Christian Science.

Ironically, in contrast to Eddy's assertions, Christian Science does teach things that one would classify as "that which is . . . human": spiritually-grounded moral principles that regulate human behavior, including ideals of selfless love preached by Jesus, as represented by the Golden Rule and the parable of the Good Samaritan. Christian Science teaches people to esteem integrity and righteous (but not self-righteous) thought and action, and encourages people to resist temptation and vice.

But Eddy didn't plumb and elucidate the profound and inescapable underlying principles that shape the patterns and conduct of our earthly adventure. True to her word, she didn't teach in any explicit and significant way that which is human. Yet statements throughout her book cause faithful adherents of Christian Science to wrongly infer that there isn't a clear, must-know architecture to the arc and chapters of our human lives.

Enter the great anthropologist and mythologist Joseph Campbell, who discovered through his study of human cultures a universal story inscribed deeply within everyone. In *The Hero with a Thousand Faces*, first published in 1949, he identified and categorized the stages of this universal journey and its archetypal cast of characters. Campbell mapped core concepts of how human life works. His research gives people today a practical field manual for understanding and leading their own lives, heightening their comprehension of what's going on and why, and what to do about it—and how and when to do it. What Campbell discovered about the universal story helps people successfully confront adversity and weather the storms we encounter as we sail toward well being, worthy achievement, selfless service, and other good goals.

"Mortal existence is an enigma," Eddy concluded. "Every day is a mystery" (*Science and Health*, p. 70). True on one level: How mortal existence can show up on the cosmic radar of reality—even as an illusion (Christian Science maintains that mortal existence is an illusion)—is indeed a mystery, given the reign of an omnipotent and benevolent Spirit (God) that created a perfect, illusion-free creation (where people don't write about, let alone get fooled or affected by, the non-existent illusion of matter, evil, and mortal existence). And so, yes, chalk up every day of mortal existence in which we are aware of this paradox as an enigma. Because in light of such sticky metaphysical mind loops, "Every day is a mystery" for sure!

But on another level, Eddy's two statements can mislead, because at best they are ambiguous and can therefore imply that the journey through life on Earth doesn't conform to reliable, timeless principles, whereas such principles do exist, revealing that our everyday lives unfold in ways that are no mystery at all. Mortal life plays out according to clear and meaningful organizing concepts. But this reality runs contrary to Eddy's implication that the way Earth life works is mysterious and has no comprehensible design, no rhyme or reason, save, it seems, to provide a baffling game board on which we, as perfect spiritual beings (offspring of Spirit), must oddly travel from "cross to crown," metaphors Eddy adopted to express the transformation everyone must undergo in consciousness along the spectrum from mortal illusion (of which human life is part) to spiritual reality (present here and now)—a paradoxical, Möbius strip-like mind-bender, collaging the illusion of mortal existence with the actuality of spiritual existence, guaranteed to make pretty much anybody's head spin.

Eddy's concept of a transformational cross-to-crown journey heralded Campbell's discovery of the Hero's Journey. But Eddy didn't unpack the archetypal human journey. She didn't outline or detail its universal design. Unlike Campbell, she didn't see that a cogent GPS system structures and signposts the highway of mortal existence. Eddy gives sailors a map of the night sky and points us to the North Star, but she doesn't give us a map of the earth.

INVISIBLE PRISON BARS

"You don't see your prison because its bars are invisible," writes Dan Millman in his terrific book *The Way of the Peaceful Warrior*. As a lifelong student of Christian Science, I've seen how the study of Christian Science can bring healing and freedom but, ironically, at the same time create invisible prison bars for people, impeding their maturity, self-awareness, discernment, freedom, and happiness. *Metaphysical Warrior* represents my prison break. Not from Christian Science—from false and limiting concepts about Christian Science, like the concepts I explained above. I also look for ways to break free from the invisible prison bars of jargon, which can contribute to a sincere Christian Scientist's oblivious imprisonment. And I count among the many books that have helped me on my quest Fredric Jameson's *The Prison-House of Language*.

Jameson delves into esoteric issues of literary theory, including aspects that dovetail with my professional research into modern theories of painting and architecture. But you can get the takeaway that I want to emphasize here from the book's title: Don't let language lock you in a prison cell of pre-programmed, mind-numbing, sleepwalking thought-speak. Escape! Find fresh, original, *unfamiliar* ways to convey *familiar* ideas.

Wake up.

As a writer and editor for nine years for *The Christian Science Journal* and *Christian Science Sentinel*—sister magazines of *The Christian Science Monitor*—I took that language challenge to heart. And I still do. I push back against routine, inside vocabulary. I try to use ordinary words to express extraordinary concepts. Throughout *Metaphysical Warrior*, I seek to honor the value of words and the truth-seeking creativity of a spiritual explorer who hopes to convey fresh insights into how we can effectively apply the spiritual metaphysics of Christian Science to our everyday lives.

I regard my commitment to this goal as honoring the spirit of Mary Baker Eddy's ongoing, implicit call to people everywhere, including, perhaps above all, adherents of Christian Science: "**The time for thinkers has come**" (*Science and Health*, p. vii).

Metaphysical Warrior seeks to honor this ideal, exemplified by Eddy herself: *thinking*—brave, independent thought in earnest pursuit of clarity and truth. Which is needed no less for the ongoing investigation and practice of Christian Science than for the ongoing investigation and practice of mathematics. Just as mathematicians seek not to undermine mathematics but to honor it by their creative search and research, so too do I seek not to undermine Christian Science but to honor it by the unique perspective that I present in this book.

By the way, I've found that when you break out of the prison-house of language, fresh winds gust through your life. You feel like you've had a mental makeover. Familiar ideas take on new meaning, a whole new look.

Someone once said that new vocabularies open up new realities. True! Catch a glimpse of those new realities, and you never want to go back to prison. You love your freedom. Freedom brings truth, as surely as truth brings freedom.

BEYOND WORDS

Mary Baker Eddy mined the Bible and landed on seven synonyms for God—Truth, Life, Mind, Spirit, Love, Soul, Principle. These synonyms open up new realities ("new realities" as old as the Bible) for anyone looking to get acquainted with God. Getting acquainted with God as Mind and Soul and Love can transform your life and bring well-being. I've experienced rescue from all kinds of adversity.

Those seven iconic English words for God strike a deep chord. We feel their power. They get us in touch with divine reality. But doesn't divine reality transcend words?

The links between human-created words and spiritual concepts, between human language and divine reality, are random. For example, no set-in-stone cosmic truth, inscribed by God, pins the Arabic-derived letters *c-a-t*, for example, to the animal that English speakers have learned to associate with those letters. That association is arbitrary. Speakers of other languages use different signs—different letters and words, different sounds and symbols—to refer to the same animal. Cats exist outside of language. So do we: so does the spiritual reality that we represent, signified by Eddy's seven synonyms for God.

Words may provide necessary basis for getting a clear handle on God, but do they provide a sufficient basis? Or do we more fully understand the nature of God (the substance and source of our being, our nature, identity, individuality) through feeling the total presence and power of all-encompassing goodness that special words hint at? After all, our scientific, coexistent relationship with our universal Soul, Principle, Mind, and Life exists beyond the prison-house of human language.

As we zoom out even more, we might ask ourselves if we truly believe that the Master Plan of Reality rests on words, let alone words that have been devised during the ephemeral condition of human experience. Do seven Planet-Earth words, in particular, enjoy special status as descriptors of the metaphysical foundation of the World?

The divine Architect, for which we've invented the word *G-o-d*, has not carved Bible-based words over the door of the Cosmos. The Arabic-derived letters that form the English words *G-o-d* or *T-r-u-t-h* or *S-p-i-r-i-t* and the words themselves are arbitrary, human-invented signs, having no intrinsic link to the profound concepts that these letters and words represent.

Read *Science and Health* and you'll see that Eddy herself cracks the door open to words for God other than those iconic seven, including good, grace, sustaining infinite, and intelligence. And are these really the only other words for God?

We need words, but I think that we also need more than words. We need a leap of intuition about the full nature of *Good in every conceivable form*.

I will continue to tap the practical power that flows from a grasp of Eddy's seven synonyms for God, and I will continue to make sound, nuanced distinctions about the meaning of words. But I am also trying to get more in touch with what Derek Linn, author of *The Tao of Daily Life*, calls a "wordless perception of reality."

NUMBERS AND NUMERALS

That said, a wordless *education* about reality will not likely take us very far. Especially when it comes to understanding the crucial interaction between our humanity and our divinity.

Think of this interaction as similar to the interaction between numbers and numerals. Remember math class in elementary school? We learned that numbers are ideas and that numerals represent those ideas through a visible sign, through a tangible expression of the idea. And that expression can assume many forms. Take the number nine. The black-ink 9 that you see here on the page? That's the numeral. Which is just one way of expressing the concept or idea of nine, the number nine. Think of some of the other countless (pun intended) "numerical" expressions of the number nine: IX, 4+5, 15-6, $\sqrt{81}$, ⦀⦀⦀ ⦀⦀⦀⦀, or Δ, in the Greek acrophonic system used in the first millennium BCE.

You can do all kinds of things to a numeral: erase it, distort it, burn it up (toss this book in the fireplace, and you'll see what I mean). But you can't do any of that to a number. Nine is an idea: lasting, permanent, durable. (Worth noting: the word *nine* in Chinese is a homophone of the word that means "longlasting.") You cannot erase, distort, or burn up (or burn out), tire, retire, harm, or kill the number nine.

What are you and I: number or numeral? Well, at our core, number. But at the same time, both—number and numeral. Paradoxically, our identity is both number-like *and* number-and-numeral-like.

Eddy discovered the inherent, indestructible *number-like identity of our spirituality*—our divinity. A divinity as present here and now as the indestructible number nine. Which means that like the number nine, you and I are an idea, and therefore everlasting, permanent, durable.

And Eddy and Campbell both caught sight of the *numeral-like essence of our humanity*, which shines most brightly when infused with the recognition of our divinity.

Referring to Jesus, Eddy said: "Through the magnitude of his human life, he demonstrated the divine Life." Jesus role-modeled the divinity-inspired humanity of the metaphysical warrior. And he said you and I have the potential to do what he did, even greater works.

So ideally, in some degree, we too can represent the vivid presence of divine Life through the magnitude of our human life. Ideally, in some degree, we too can role-model the divinity-inspired humanity of the metaphysical warrior.

3-D METAPHYSICAL WARRIOR

In the foreword to Steven Pressfield's *The War of Art*, Robert McKee, author of *Story*, defines talent: "the innate power to discover the hidden connection between two things—images, ideas, words—that no one else has ever seen before, link them, and create for the world a third, utterly unique work."

Mary Baker Eddy did that. Ancient Greek and Enlightenment philosophers, as well as 19th-century Transcendentalists, saw an invisible plane of reality behind the facade of human life. Plato in antiquity and Descartes in the 17th century at the beginning of the Enlightenment regarded the human soul and mind as immaterial, spiritual. And Enlightenment philosopher Bishop Berkeley denied the *entire* existence of matter. In his essay "The Over-Soul" (1841), Emerson painted a picture of "the eternal ONE," proclaiming that "this deep power in which we exist and whose beatitude is all accessible to us, is not only self-sufficing and perfect in every hour, but the act of seeing and the thing seen, the seer and the spectacle, the subject and the object, are one."

Many of these people influenced Eddy's thinking. But Eddy saw something they didn't. She explored paths her brothers in metaphysics didn't travel (yes, they were all men). She saw how the ancient Hebrews had a concept of God they equated with the "holy Spirit." She saw that other aspects of God's nature could be drawn from the Bible's deep well—and therefore capitalized: Mind, Soul, Principle, Life, for example. And she put these absolutes together with what she learned from Bible stories of divine healing of the human body and spiritual transformation of human events to create, in 1866, a third new, original thing: Christian Science—her discovery of the scientific law by which alignment with divine reality brings health and wholeness to human life, including the physical body. In other words, Eddy discovered that tuning into the behind-the-scenes reality of Emerson's "eternal ONE" can yield *practical power*.

So far, Jesus has best exemplified this practical power. Through precision alignment with Truth, Life, and Love, Jesus exercised spiritual mastery over material conditions. He said, "I and my Father are one" (John 10:30). Eddy used metaphors to explain what Jesus meant: "**As a drop of water is one with the ocean, a ray of light one with the sun, even so God and man, Father and son, are one in being**" (*Science and Health*, p. 361). Jesus summoned spiritual power as surely and naturally as star beams summon star power. And Eddy emphasized throughout *Science and Health* that everyone has the potential to experience the practical power that flows from an immanent sense of oneness with our universal Principle, Soul, and Mind.

Eddy's simile for our scientific unity with spiritual reality—as "a ray of light one with the sun"— struck a chord in me long ago. I get how a sunbeam enjoys scientific unity with the sun. After dark, on a clear night, I look for Sirius, the brightest star in the night sky. I remind myself that in the same way that a ray of starlight coexists with a star, I coexist with Mind. And so does everyone. This simile sums up, so simply, our direct and inseparable relationship to Life and Mind and Soul, and to everything else that is good. And this simile plays a starring role in *Metaphysical Warrior*.

As to my talent? The McKee-defined talent on which I base this book and my life? Putting together the discoveries of Eddy and the discoveries of Campbell to create a third, new thing: the concept of a metaphysical warrior—specifically, the concept of a full-fledged 3-D Metaphysical Warrior who peacefully, trenchantly, and fruitfully sojourns in the land of existence by embracing the dynamic relationship between the archetypal design of human life and the ideal design of divine Life. My quest to understand the architecture of experience has brought me to this plateau—to a clear view of the practical software of the 3-D Metaphysical Warrior, humanly self-aware and spiritually enlightened. I don't know a better way to hold on as we hurtle through the Universe in the Milky Way Galaxy on what Buckminster Fuller called "Spaceship Earth."

MASTERS OF ADVERSITY

The essays and collection of random notes in this book reflect my personal fusion of the human life principles discovered by Campbell and the divine Life-Principle discovered by Eddy.

I've adopted for my life-journey this slogan—Eddy's seven-word imperative, which one day jumped off page 419 of *Science and Health* and into my soul: "**Meet every adverse circumstance as its master.**"

Metaphysical Warrior distills what I have learned through decades of study and experience that helps me do this. And I hope that something I say will help you master adversity in your life, as you seek fulfillment of your endeavors, goals, and dreams.

PUBLIC

GROW UP.

Journey Through The Labyrinth

Everything we need for our Adventure lies within our reach.

1

PUBLIC

METAPHYSICAL WARRIOR

WE HAVE NOT EVEN TO RISK THE ADVENTURE ALONE; FOR THE HEROES OF ALL TIME HAVE GONE BEFORE US; THE LABYRINTH IS THOROUGHLY KNOWN; WE HAVE ONLY TO FOLLOW THE THREAD OF THE HERO-PATH. —Joseph Campbell

As you read those lines, travel back to a time thousands of years ago to the Mediterranean island of Crete and to the mythical kingdom of King Minos.

And picture a labyrinth—a maze of elaborate complexity where, in its heart, dwells a savage beast with the head of a bull and the body of a man: the Minotaur.

Every year, to avenge the murder of his son by the Athenians, King Minos sends seven Athenian young men and seven Athenian young women into the labyrinth for the Minotaur to devour.

Enter Theseus, the mythical King of Athens, who sails to Crete to slay the Minotaur and put a stop to King Minos's brutality.

Theseus possesses the courage and strength of a hero. But he will need more than those two essential qualities to win the day. And as he will discover, events transpire behind the scenes to equip him with everything else he will need to fulfill his quest.

Princess Ariadne, Minos's daughter, falls in love with the handsome Theseus the moment she sees him disembark from the boat that brings him to Crete. Fearing for his life, Ariadne turns for help to the architect of the labyrinth, Daedalus.

Daedalus spins a spool of thread and gives it to Ariadne with these directions: "Tell Theseus to tie one end of the thread to the entrance of the labyrinth and unspool the thread as he winds his way to the center. After he slays the monster, he can then follow the thread back out to safety."

Ariadne gives Theseus the spool of thread and relays Daedalus's directions. She also gives Theseus a sword. Equipped with Daedalus's thread and Ariadne's sword, Theseus triumphs.

METAPHOR AND MEANING

Ancient Greek storytellers crafted myths to convey their insights about the drama, emotions, and symbolic patterns of life. Like all great works of fiction, these Greek myths teach lessons that continue to have timeless relevance to our everyday lives.

In his book *The Hero With A Thousand Faces,* 20th-century anthropologist Joseph Campbell unpacked the ancient Greek myth of the labyrinth. Drawing from years of research into this and countless other myths, as well as stories about central figures and events in many cultures around the world, Campbell identified a universal set of archetypal concepts that describe the design and conduct of life. He called this set of archetypal concepts, "The Hero's Journey."

Thanks to Campbell, I now read into the ancient Greek myth of the labyrinth and its cast of characters layers of metaphor and meaning that enrich my life and work. I've created several paintings that I call *Labyrinth*, including the one that introduces this essay. I just finished a book on architecture and painting called *Daedalus 9*. My creation of that book took me through every phase and stage of the Hero's Journey. I'm now working on a building that I title *The Daedalus Project: The Hero's Journey House*. I see already how the project is unfolding in ways that follow the patterns of the Hero's Journey. And as I write this book—and this chapter, especially—I observe how my path has conformed to the same template.

Equally important, the concepts of the Hero's Journey help me in practical ways in other areas of my life, from my relationships with friends, coworkers, and family to my physical and spiritual health.

Thanks to Campbell's own hero's journey, which resulted in the publication of his books, I now see that I am the hero in the story of my own life—just as you are the hero in the story of your own life.

THE HERO'S JOURNEY

The Hero's Journey represents the struggle and transformation people must undergo when they pursue their hopes and dreams or when they must face trouble that gets thrust upon them. Key aspects of our lives tend to play out according to this age-old paradigm of the Hero's Journey, which Campbell described on page 3 of *The Hero With A Thousand Faces* as "the one, shape-shifting yet marvelously constant story."

When we learn the simple structure and characters of this constant story, our life-IQ shoots up. We feel less baffled, frustrated, resentful, or afraid in the face of overwhelming challenges and disheartening adversities. We no longer drive through a strange landscape without a map—

we have a universal, reliable GPS. We can access the overview and look ahead. Knowledge of how life works and what we will likely encounter along our journey equips us to move forward through tests and tribulations with uncanny perspective and wisdom. Allies come to our aid in the form of golden faculties that include intuition and foresight, poise, resilience, and tenacity. And my favorite—grit—which the dictionary defines as "firmness of mind or spirit—unyielding courage in the face of hardship or danger."

In *The Hero With A Thousand Faces*, Campbell identified and explained "The Adventure of the Hero," breaking down this Adventure—the Hero's Journey—into 17 stages that span the three basic phases of a story: beginning, middle, and end. Campbell termed these three phases, "Departure, Initiation, Return." Hollywood story consultant Christopher Vogler collapsed Campbell's 17 stages into 12 stages in his book *The Writer's Journey*, one of the cornerstones of modern screenwriting theory.

Below, I show Vogler's 12 stages as they fall within the outline of Campbell's three basic phases of a story. But instead of "Initiation," I call the second phase, "Transformation"—the part of the story when the hero journeys through "The Labyrinth," which takes a different form from story to story. And remember, when we realize the Adventure of the Hero describes the inevitable arc of various chapters of your life-story, this arc becomes a vital, practical tool to comprehend and navigate our own human Adventure.

DEPARTURE—From the Ordinary World
1. Ordinary World
2. Call to Adventure
3. Refusal of the Call
4. Meeting with the Mentor
5. Crossing the First Threshold

TRANSFORMATION—In the Special World (The Labyrinth)
6. Test, Allies, Enemies
7. Approach to the Inmost Cave
8. Ordeal
9. Reward (Seizing the Sword)

RETURN—To the Ordinary World
10. The Road Back
11. Resurrection
12. Return with the Elixir

In Chapter 9, I will give an example of how I moved through these three phases and simultaneously through the 12 stages of the Hero's Journey during a recent episode in my life.

Campbell also identifies the typical cast of the Hero's Journey. In addition to Hero, the basic roles that people play in each other's lives include Mentor, Threshold Guardian, Herald, Shapeshifter, Shadow, and Trickster.

If you view the world through this marvelous lens, you will see that the 12 stages and seven character types of the Hero's Journey provide the framework for the story lines of countless Hollywood movies, like the story line of the movie that Vogler analyzes in *The Writer's Journey* to illustrate the Hero's Journey, *The Wizard of Oz*.

More important, the Hero's Journey provides the framework for the lives of significant real-life people throughout history—from explorers, scientists, philosophers, athletes, and artists to political, business, and religious leaders.

But perhaps most important, I believe, the Hero's Journey also provides the framework for your life and mine. Every knock of opportunity and desire to create or do something worthwhile, as well as every unwelcome contest with trouble, signals us to prepare for **DEPARTURE** from our **Ordinary World** of limited perceptions, deficient wisdom, lack of experience, or dormant talents that could revive us and help others. After much soul-searching and doubt, we may resist change so much that we say "no" to the **Call to Adventure**. But we get a new perspective from our **Meeting with the Mentor**. The Mentor may be a wiser, more experienced person, a book, or the counsel that comes to us through meditation, intuition, or prayer. The Mentor urges, "Go. We are called only to adventures that we are ready for. You are ready without knowing it."

I have found in many situations that my Meeting with the Mentor takes place by turning inward to Spirit, and what I need to know often comes to me as a line from the Bible. This passage, for example—Exodus 23:20—has given me the assurance to move forward at crucial times in my life when I felt reluctant to do so: "Behold, I send an Angel before thee, to keep thee in the way, and to bring thee into the place which I have prepared."

Many people find, as I do, that Meeting with the Mentor can take place when they draw inspiration from the spirit and consciousness of heroes who have gone before us, like mountaineer W. H. Murray, who wrote these famous lines in his 1951 chronicle, *The Scottish Himalayan Expedition* (p. 7): "Until one is committed, there is hesitancy, the chance to draw back, always ineffectiveness. Concerning all acts of initiative (and creation), there is one elementary truth the ignorance of which kills countless ideas and splendid plans: that the moment one definitely commits oneself, then providence moves too. A whole stream of events issues from the decision, raising in one's favor all manner of unforeseen incidents, meetings and material assistance, which no man could have dreamt would have come his way. I learned a deep respect for one of Goethe's couplets: 'Whatever you can do or dream you can, begin it. / Boldness has genius, power and magic in it'."

And who cannot experience a decisive Meeting-with-the-Mentor moment when we feel the heart-pounding truth of Joseph Campbell's insight in *The Hero With A Thousand Faces* (p. 25), "We have not even to risk the adventure alone; for the heroes of all time have gone before us; the labyrinth is thoroughly known; we have only to follow the thread of the hero-path."

But whatever way we experience our special Meeting with the Mentor, afterward we feel ready to say "yes" to our Adventure. And with newfound clarity, heart, and resolve, through inspiration or simple determination, we take our first brave step toward a goal—whether to start a business, get a college degree, write a book, make a film, build a house, become a chef, run for office, win a court case, get a divorce, find physical, emotional, or financial healing. When we take that brave step, we will find ourselves **Crossing the First Threshold** into a new and challenging, sometimes scary and disorienting, Special World.

In this Special World, which I designate The Labyrinth phase of our journey, we will experience a **TRANSFORMATION** as we make our way with various forms of help through different levels of resistance (**Tests, Allies, Enemies**). Our **Approach to the Inmost Cave**—the heart of The Labyrinth—makes us realize that achieving our quest will likely require far more than we bargained for and thought we were capable of. But new energy, wit, and inspiration inevitably comes to our aid. For example, we might recall the eternal promise of Virgil's *The Aeneid*, "The path of safety will open up for you from where you least imagine it." And we press on.

And as we do, we will enlist more Allies and encounter more Enemies (Threshold Guardians, Shapeshifters, Shadows, and Tricksters) as we make our way through The Labyrinth. These can be coworkers, lovers, parents, managers, publishers, teachers, bosses, rivals, friends, or children. But each one has a significant role to play.

Eventually, we come face to face with the **Ordeal** that requires all of our resources, skills, dedication, and strength to endure and prevail. A supreme test of our convictions and character, the Ordeal is the Minotaur that we must slay to achieve our goal—our **Reward**—which requires **Seizing the Sword**. For example, for Theseus the Reward for slaying the Minotaur was the rescue of young Greek men and women and consequently the safeguarding of the future of Greek society.

Sooner or later along our Adventure, we realize that the archetypal Hero's Journey not only takes us on an outer quest for victory, but also on an inner quest for enlightenment. So the Ordeal also requires Seizing the Sword to slay the inner monster—which can take the form of doubt, discouragement, immaturity, superstition, a crisis of integrity or faith, whatever our greatest fear is—that stands in the way of our outer victory and a more fully-evolved inner self.

The time frame of the Ordeal that leads to Reward can vary widely. For example, it could last as long as the 9.63 seconds that it took for Usain Bolt to win the 100 meter dash and claim the gold medal in the 2012 Summer Olympics, or as long as the three sets of tennis it took for Billie Jean King to beat Bobby Riggs in the crucial turning point in the history of women's tennis, the famed "Battle of the Sexes" in 1973. The Ordeal could take as long as the 20 days that it took Jack Kerouac to write the first draft of *On the Road* in 1951 (after he spent years writing notes and outlining the book), or as long as the first seven years that mathematician Andrew Wiles spent working on the proof of Fermat's Last Theorem leading to his public announcement in 1993 that he had succeeded. The Ordeal could take as long as the three days that Jesus spent in the tomb facing down the Minotaur of death—after the 12 hours of arrest, trial, and crucifixion that he endured on his Approach to the Inmost Cave. Or the Ordeal could take as long as the some six years between 1869 and 1875 that Mary Baker Eddy spent writing the first edition of *Science and Health with Key to the Scriptures*, in which she disclosed her discovery of the universal Life-Principle underlying Jesus's victory over death.

However long the Ordeal takes, after winning the desired prize of our quest, we head home: We begin our **RETURN**. **The Road Back** may not be easy—physically or emotionally—often requiring that we pass one last, final exam. We may face a final "brush with death"—a false death, as it were. But we prevail. Gaining mastery of our faculties and capacities, as well as awareness of our true self and nature, we experience a **Resurrection**.

Finally, our quest complete, we **Return with the Elixir** of wisdom and inspiration to lead lives enriched and strengthened by our adventure, imparting to others the hard-earned insights of our journey.

Consider the breathtaking example of Andrew Wiles. Fermat's Last Theorem had fascinated Wiles since childhood, when he first dreamed of devising a proof for the celebrated theorem conjectured by Pierre de Fermat in 1637. Starting in 1986, Wiles worked tirelessly and in near-total secrecy for seven years on this mathematical enigma, which had defied all previous attempts by mathematicians to solve for over 350 years. He presented his proof to the public in 1993, thinking that he had seized his Reward. But The Road Back turned into a nightmare. Other mathematicians soon discovered a flaw in one area of the proof. For over a year, Wiles tried and failed to correct this flawed area. We can only imagine his despair. In fact, Wiles says that the crucial idea of how to circumvent rather than resolve this flawed area came to him on September 19, 1994, when he was on the verge of giving up.

In the classic pattern of the Adventure of the Hero on The Road Back, Andrew Wiles experienced an emotional and intellectual near-death experience. But he survived it. Moving through this Resurrection stage,

Wiles, together with his former student Richard Taylor, published the completed proof in 1995 in a special volume of the *Annals of Mathematics*, marking Wiles's triumphant Return with the Elixir and the end of his heroic nine-year journey.

LABYRINTHS WITHIN THE LABYRINTH

Daedalus and Theseus each took a hero's journey that fits the pattern I've described. Their lives converged at the labyrinth of Crete. I continue to find great practical meaning in the ancient Greek myth of the labyrinth and the roles of Daedalus and Theseus—and Ariadne. The brief story of how this trio banded together to slay the Minotaur offers an array of insights into the Hero's Journey of life and gives me new angles for viewing and understanding the architecture of existence. My insights build on those of Campbell and Vogler and arise from my perspective as a Christian Scientist.

I think of the labyrinth as a metaphor for our human experience. On one level, the labyrinth serves as a metaphor for human experience overall, during which we undergo Transformation as we navigate life from entrance to exit. On another level, the labyrinth serves as a metaphor for the adversities and ordeals that we face within our human experience, those disorienting and distressing testing times of our lives during which we undergo Transformation after Transformation as we pursue goals and welcome opportunities or confront unwanted challenges. And I've learned that if we want to successfully navigate a labyrinth, we must do as Theseus did and follow Daedalus's thread—a metaphor, as Campbell explains, for the "hero-path."

Campbell saw, as the ancient Greeks saw before him, that our voluntary and involuntary journeys toward goals, resolution, harmony, and change—in whatever aspect of human life—can feel very much like a journey through a labyrinth: baffling, dark, lacking order and coherence, uncharted, nonparadgimatic, unnavigable, an enigma. We may get the false impression that the way our lives unfold through welcome opportunities or unwelcome trouble cannot be neatly classified, easily understood, and wisely anticipated. This false impression disables us. It cuts us off from a tremendous source of perspicacity, wisdom, and power that can shape our decisions and conduct.

But as it turns out, and as Theseus learned from Daedalus (by way of Ariadne), a labyrinth isn't hard to understand or explain. A labyrinth, however elaborate and complex, appears to be an enigma only to those who don't have a blueprint—or, worse yet, to those who don't even know that they are in a labyrinth.

A labyrinth is typically a well-designed coherent structure, a rational construction that springs from the mind of an architect, who can easily unlock the labyrinth's apparent mystery. And so Campbell, mirroring the role of architect—a modern-day Daedalus—rolls out the blueprint of the iconic and universal human journey, revealing that it is as organized, predictable, and conventional as the arrangement of the floor plan of a traditional house, assuring us that plainly "the labyrinth is thoroughly known; we have only to follow the thread of the hero-path."

Just as Daedalus showed Theseus the hero-path through the physical labyrinth, Campbell shows us the hero-path through the figurative labyrinth. His book *The Hero With A Thousand Faces* is our Daedalus's thread—or at least very special strands of Daedalus's thread.

Now, to clarify: The hero-path winds through all the stages of the Hero's Journey, from Departure to Transformation to Return. For example, Theseus's adventure along the hero-path began before and continued after he followed Daedalus's thread through the labyrinth. Theseus's hero-path began with his Departure from Athens, and he traveled this hero-path through his Transformation in Crete and his Return to Athens.

I designate the middle phase of a story not only as Transformation, but also as The Labyrinth. So for Theseus, Crete was The Labyrinth phase of his story (the Special World versus the Ordinary World of Athens). And within The Labyrinth phase, Theseus encountered in Crete a *physical labyrinth* designed and built by Daedalus. Through a simple spool of thread, Daedalus showed Theseus the hero-path through that physical labyrinth—and only through that physical labyrinth, not through any other part of Theseus's Athens-to-Crete-to-Athens journey.

But Campbell's insights expand the metaphorical significance of Daedalus's thread to include the hero-path through the *entire* Hero's Journey. Though unlike me, Campbell refers to the thread of the hero-path as "Ariadne's thread," not "Daedalus's thread."

Wrapping your head around this concept of a labyrinth within a labyrinth can start to make you feel like you're in a labyrinth, I know! But I believe that this concept applies to our lives.

Human existence is a Labyrinth. Over the course of our human lives, we adventure through many labyrinths within this Labyrinth. We make our way as best we can from the time we enter the Labyrinth of human existence to the time we leave it—from the point at which we appear on Earth to the point at which we disappear from Earth. Along the way, we experience different types of labyrinths—intellectual, physical, psychological, emotional, financial, political, professional, interpersonal, intrapersonal—that make up the overlapping chapters in the unique story of our lives. The concepts of the Hero's Journey that Campbell discovered can help us thread our way through the Labyrinth of human existence and through the labyrinths within this Labyrinth.

But to prevail, I have learned that we need more than the brilliant and practical insights revealed in *The Hero With A Thousand Faces* and enlarged by Vogler in *The Writer's Journey*. "It is, indeed, very little that we need!" writes Campbell. "But lacking that, the adventure into the labyrinth is without hope" (p. 23). We need more than a blueprint, more than a clear, well-marked, and inevitable hero-path. We also need the other strands of Daedalus's thread.

STRANDS OF DAEDALUS'S THREAD

The way I see it, Daedalus's thread is primarily a metaphor for intelligence.

After all, isn't that what Ariadne actually sought to obtain from Daedalus? The intelligence needed for someone to safely navigate the labyrinth? And he gave it to her in the clever form of a spool of thread. In fact, the Greek word *Daedalus* means "clever worker"—and *clever* means "mentally quick and resourceful, showing intelligent thinking."

Think of Daedalus's thread as comprising countless strands, and some of the strands represent the concepts of the hero-path and Hero's Journey, equipping us with an outline and guiding principles for our quest—even an outlook, or higher consciousness. And experience has taught me that I would not want to live without this valuable assistance. I regard this form of assistance—these strands of Daedalus's thread—as human intelligence.

But experience has also taught me to rely on another, deeper source of intelligence as I travel through my hero's journey.

For example, let's say that I follow my iPhone GPS on my drive from Los Angeles to Sacramento and feel totally confident that I won't get lost and will arrive home safely. But neither my confidence (my outlook) nor the GPS will tell me if, when, and where I ought to stop for food and fuel, when to slow down or speed up and in which lane, whether to brave the downpour or pull off to the side and wait. GPS and self-confidence won't prompt me to call someone or send an important text message along the way. For that kind of help, I need some other kind of decision-making paradigm. I need to rely on the other facet of intelligence that, as I see it, Daedalus symbolically provided Ariadne and that she in turn provided Theseus. This form of intelligence helped him unspool the thread the right way through the Labyrinth, governed his timing, intuition, and other faculties of his conduct and character, ensuring that he indeed could complete his mission and safely exit the labyrinth without getting confused and lost.

I regard this form of assistance along the hero-path—these other strands of Daedalus's thread—as spiritual intelligence.

SPIRITUAL INTELLIGENCE

And where do we turn for spiritual intelligence? Not to the fictional architect, Daedalus. But to the real Architect, divine Mind. And for this enlightenment, I thank the author of *Science and Health* and the discoverer of Christian Science, Mary Baker Eddy.

Based on her lifelong study of the Bible, Eddy defined God as Mind—and Mind as God. She capitalized *Mind* to signify this. I've learned in so many vivid ways throughout my life, that even as we pass through the darkest passages of the labyrinth of human experience, we can rely on our divine Mind—the one universal Mind—to guide us. As the Bible assures, "And the Lord [Mind] shall guide thee continually" (Isa. 58:11). Divine Mind continuously refreshes and sustains us on our journey, supplying the spiritual qualities that we need to cut through the labyrinth of despair, fear, naivete, and confusion.

I think of spiritual qualities in simple terms as qualities that we do not see with our eyes, but qualities that we can distinguish from physical qualities such as height, weight, and appearance. Chief among these spiritual qualities is intelligence. Eddy refers to intelligence on page 469 of *Science and Health* as "the primal and eternal quality of infinite Mind, of the triune Principle,—Life, Truth, and Love,—named God."

I looked up the word *intelligence* many years ago and learned that it derives from the Latin verb *intelligere*, meaning "to choose between."

I remember thinking, *So intelligence, the primary quality of God, the essential quality not only of Mind but also of Life and even of Love, is the basic ability to "choose"—in other words, to make good choices. Wow. Of course! I face choices almost every second. My whole life is about choices.*

I began to think about intelligence from this new angle—the Mind-sourced capacity to *make good choices*. And my life began to move forward in surprising ways. For example, though a licensed architect, I chose to take a course at Columbia University, during the summer of 2001, on screenwriting. Taught by David McKenna, this course introduced me to the ideas of Christopher Vogler and Joseph Campbell. I learned about the screenplay of my own life, about its discernible, coherent architecture and archetypal dramatic structure—launching me on an adventure to become the person I could not at the time foresee: a metaphysical warrior.

We can acquire knowledge and excel academically, take a deep dive into ideas, and even become nimble, abstract thinkers. And I value these aspects of intelligence. But at root, intelligence is primarily our capacity to rise above confusion and correctly choose between two things that vie for our attention—typically, after choosing among many things our favorite two. We all face the same basic choices: A or B. Yes or no. Right or wrong. Now or later. *This way or that way.* And these choices involve food, time, money, school, work, love—and everything in between.

So when I face a choice, and I seek clarity about which way to go, I turn to the source of unerring intelligence: infinite Mind.

Here's what works for me: I take 20 seconds to close my eyes and affirm the truth of Psalms 71:1: "In thee, O Lord [Mind], do I put my trust: let me never be put to confusion." My translation:

> I know what to do, and I know how to do it; I know what to say, and I know how to say it; I know if to do it and when to do it—because I coexist with and express Mind as a sunbeam coexists with and expresses the sun. What goes for me goes for everyone.

And I always follow that up with this tagline:

That's the truth. And I expect proof.

MIND AS MENTOR

The word *mind* derives from the same root word as the word *mentor*. We get the word *mentor* from Greek myth: Mentor was a friend of Odysseus, the hero of the Greek epic The Odyssey. Mentor was entrusted with the education of Odysseus's son Telemachus. The dictionary defines *mentor* as "a trusted counselor or guide."

In a deeply metaphysical but immediately practical sense, Mind is our Mentor, our trusted Counselor and Guide. And our Meeting with the Mentor doesn't happen only during stage four of the Departure phase of the Hero's Journey. We can companion with Mind continuously along the way from start to finish. With every step we take through one kind of labyrinth or another, we can feel the presence of Mind steering us forward.

Truly, we do not risk the adventure alone.

ARIADNE'S SWORD

Like Theseus, if we hope to survive our own labyrinth, we would be wise to take not only Daedalus's thread: the intertwined strands of human and spiritual intelligence to which we all have access in the form of the principles of the Hero's Journey and the continuous mentoring power of divine Mind. We would also be wise to take a sword.

Not the sword referred to in stage 9 in the Hero's Journey (Seizing the Sword)—but the sword that Ariadne gave Theseus to take with him into the Labyrinth.

But what is Ariadne's sword? What does it stand for?

I recently delved more deeply into the meaning of a line by Joseph Campbell on page 24 of *The Hero With A Thousand Faces*: "[Daedalus] is the hero of the way of thought—singlehearted, courageous, and full of faith that the truth, as he finds it, shall make us free. And so now we may turn to him, as did Ariadne. The flax for the linen of his thread he has gathered from the fields of the human imagination."

These lines not only expanded my appreciation for the evocative and practical symbolism of Daedalus's thread. They also increased my appreciation of the symbolic value of Daedalus himself and led me to an insight about Ariadne's sword.

I was struck by Campbell's poetic insights, especially by the phrase "the hero of the way of thought," which underscores his uncanny insight into the crucial role that thought plays in shaping our lives. As an architect, I took special note that Campbell equates Daedalus with the hero mentality. I realized that mythical Daedalus could teach me a lot: He faced intense adversity during more than one episode in his life. The spiritual qualities that Campbell ascribes to him—unwavering purpose, bravery, and confidence in the freedom-giving power of truth—not only equipped Daedalus to help Ariadne and Theseus. These qualities, as well as innovation, creativity, and resourcefulness, also equipped Daedalus during a crucial episode when the stakes rose even higher.

Ariadne's love for Theseus helped her foresee that he would need not only the thread that Daedalus provided—intelligence. Theseus would also need a tangible symbol of the spirit of Daedalus. As I see it, Ariadne's sword is a metaphor for the hero's way of thought.

THE HERO'S WAY OF THOUGHT

For me, as a Christian Scientist, the hero's way of thought includes everything that Daedalus represents but far more. The hero's way of thought is the way of thought of a metaphysical warrior.

So when I picture the sword that Ariadne gave Theseus in the ancient Greek myth of the labyrinth—metaphorically, a universal sword that everyone can wield—I see a double-edged blade. One edge of the sword is the heroic human spirit symbolized by Daedalus and described by Joseph Campbell: "singlehearted, courageous, and full of faith that the truth, as he finds it, shall make us free." The other edge of the sword is the complementary spiritual anthem proclaimed by Mary Baker Eddy to every metaphysical warrior: "Meet every adverse circumstance as its master" (*Science and Health*, p. 419). She explains how to do this, and throughout *Metaphysical Warrior*, I explain how I apply what Eddy's book has taught me.

Without the "sword" of the metaphysical warrior's way of thought —the ultimate hero's way of thought—I don't know how I would make my way through life's Labyrinth and sub-labyrinths.

SELF-MADE LABYRINTHS

I recently caught a glimpse of other aspects of the Hero's Journey when I peeled back more layers of the Greek myth of the labyrinth, especially the parts of the myth that center on Daedalus.

And since that day, I've been turning these insights over in my mind.

In the fall of 2013, I spent an outdoor evening with friends. As we gazed at the star-jeweled sky and scanned for our favorite constellations, one friend told of her search for a key to freedom from physical pain that had started when she was 12. After searching for 10 years, she experienced a life-changing breakthrough: Her mother disclosed a trauma and fears that she had kept hidden. Upon hearing of her mother's secrets, my friend suddenly realized that her own quest for well-being was linked to her mother's quest for well-being. My friend saw that she must escape the grip of her mother's oppressive, even strangulating, fear for her daughter's safety. The fears the mother had been harboring were affecting my friend's health as well as her mother's. My friend saw that if she could find release from this unwitting oppression, perhaps her freedom could break the spell of misery for her mother.

My friend had navigated for years through the dim labyrinth of her own inner and outer life, looking for light, seeking to gather random stars into a coherent constellation. Typical of the person who follows the well-worn path of the Hero's Journey, my friend's perseverance eventually paid off. She found that light. She found healing. Her mother too felt a burden lift. And together they experienced newfound empathy, trust, and love.

Even though my friend, a Christian Scientist, hadn't consciously aligned herself with Campbell's Hero's Journey, I suspect that she progressed through its archetypal stages as humans have done for millennia.

My friend's story got my wheels turning about Daedalus. I recalled his full story, from beginning to end, and then it hit me: The hero's way of thought can help anyone who hopes to thread successfully through the shape-shifting labyrinths of human experience—including not only the labyrinths that others or other forces create, which the stories of my friend and the mythical Theseus illustrate, but also the labyrinths that we ourselves create, which the story of the mythical Daedalus illustrates. For as it turns out, Daedalus not only helped rescue Theseus from the labyrinth—Daedalus also rescued himself from the labyrinth.

The story goes: After Theseus slays the Minotaur, King Minos punishes Daedalus, imprisoning him, along with his son Icarus, inside a tower within the labyrinth, the very labyrinth that Daedalus had designed and built. Again undaunted, he summons courage, imagination, and ingenuity, just as he had summoned these qualities to help Ariadne rescue Theseus from certain doom. Using wax and feathers, Daedalus creates wings! And with Icarus, he flies from the tower and escapes from his self-made labyrinth.

Tragically, however, the story doesn't end here. Daedalus had warned Icarus that the wax that held his wings intact would melt if he flew too close to the sun, but reckless Icarus ignores the warning and flies higher and higher. When Icarus's wings finally collapse, dread-struck Daedalus watches helplessly as his son plunges to his death in the sea.

As we go deeper into the myth, we find that Daedalus became not only a prisoner of an outer labyrinth of his own creating—a physical labyrinth. He also became a prisoner of an inner labyrinth of his own creating—a mental labyrinth. Because before arriving in Crete, Daedalus had fallen from grace. Like Theseus, Daedalus had at one time been King of Athens. But he committed a crime. Depending on the version of the myth you read, he either fled to Crete or was banished to Crete. Either way, Crete offered him an escape from the dark nightmare of his personal tragedy and shame. I convey a version of the story of Daedalus's life before Crete in the first stanza of my poem, "Flight Master."

Daedalus murdered his sister's son Talus.
Envy of the nephew's talents spurred
Daedalus's monstrous crime.
King of Athens, the city his grandfather
Erechtheus built,
Fallen Daedalus fled to Crete for solace.

Who are you, single-hearted Daedalus?
Craftsman for Queen Pasiphaë's desire,
Designer for King Minos's wrath,
Rescuer of their daughter Ariadne's heart:
So her Theseus could slay the Minotaur,
You unspooled the secret of your Labyrinth.

How shall I know you, King Daedalus?
Creator of wings, spinner of yarns, architect,
Thought-hero of thunderous imagination,
Brave truth-seeker of art, beyond time.
Or simply as you know yourself?
Sad father who lost dear Icarus to the sun.

Alternate versions of the Daedalus myth include several major variations about the incidents preceding his flight to Crete. In one version, King Daedalus doesn't kill his nephew, because his sister intervenes and turns her son Talus into a partridge. Yet, independent of whether Daedalus does or doesn't kill Talus, in another version of the myth, Daedalus's murderous passion rises not from envy of his nephew, but from outrage that his nephew takes credit for inventing a tool—the saw—that Daedalus had invented. Through this version of the myth, the ancient Greeks convey that the theft of other people's work and identity takes its toll on society and individuals. Such transgressions can stir dizzying emotions in the heart of the victim, even leading, as in the case of Daedalus, to violence and to a self-inflicted reversal of fortune.

In all versions of this myth, King Daedalus falls from grace to agony. Whether murderer or attempted murderer, whether perpetrator of a crime or the victim of a betrayal, whether fleeing Greece in shame or banished from Greece as punishment, this mighty king tumbles from the mountaintop into a labyrinth of darkness. He toils in the valley of disgrace and shame, offering his services to the dysfunctional royal household of Crete, tilling the soil of ingenuity and creativity, and ultimately spinning the thread of wisdom that saves others from doom. And even when his life takes yet another dark turn and he becomes a prisoner of his own labyrinth, Daedalus rises undaunted. He wings his way out of and above the sorrow, mistakes, and misery of his past.

ARCHITECTS OF OUR OWN ESCAPE

Through the myth of Daedalus, ancient Greek storytellers conveyed how life works: People architect their own labyrinths. Yes, we all trek through the one, universal Master Labyrinth, built from rock quarried in the deepest mines of human consciousness. But like Daedalus, we all in some sense create our own personal labyrinths, minute-by-minute, day-by-day, from the flimsy, opaque materials of our own disabling perceptions.

But any of us can emulate Daedalus's achievement and summon the wherewithal required to also architect our own escape. We may find ourselves imprisoned by labyrinths constructed of other people's impositions, envies, and false accusations, or our own under-evolved concepts of ourselves. We may feel totally lost. But we *can* escape. No matter how hard we get knocked down, no matter how far we fall, like Daedalus, we too can bounce back. We can discover new talents and resources, regain ingenuity, resilience, imagination, exhilaration, and the gifts of preparation and anticipation—we can draw on unlimited resources of Mind to bring about our rescue and set us on a course toward greater happiness, fulfillment, and freedom.

Whatever the circumstances—from romantic and family relationships to mental and physical health to finances and purpose and work—"we have not even to risk the adventure alone," as Campbell says (*The Hero With A Thousand Faces*, p. 25), because we can never be separated from the guiding and sustaining influence of Mind.

We cannot avoid the labyrinth if we hope to move forward. To create something, to make something, to achieve something worthy, you must go into the labyrinth. Because the labyrinth is where our growth and development, our progress and enlightenment take place.

That's the hero's way: We must depart from our everyday world and, as Theseus experienced in the actual labyrinth and Daedalus experienced in the major labyrinth of his life, Crete, we must each head into the fish-out-of-water strange new world of adventure, where we don't know what's around the bend or what obstacles lie in our path or what people and ideas we will encounter who will assist us along the way to our goal. And whatever the goal, whatever the challenge, test or opportunity, the journey is the same: Departure, Transformation, Return. We go into the labyrinth, and we come back out. Changed.

The adventure of the hero is always and essentially an inner quest—the road to a higher understanding of who we are, a discovery of our true selves, a transformation of the soul.

ETERNAL JOURNEY

As I explained earlier, I see the labyrinth as a metaphor for our human experience—a metaphor not only for the many overlapping chapters of our lives in which we either pursue welcome opportunities or face unwanted challenges, but also for human life overall. We navigate simultaneously labyrinths within the Labyrinth of human existence and the Labyrinth of human existence itself.

On the one hand, if we zoom in, we see that our human life includes any number of different hero's journeys, and therefore our human life unfolds through the various labyrinth experiences associated with those different hero's journeys. On the other hand, if we zoom out, we see that our entire human life, as a whole, spans the arc of a single Hero's Journey, and therefore our human life unfolds through a single, overall Labyrinth experience, framed by events in our human life that represent some form of Departure and Return.

And if we zoom out even more, if we dare to look beyond the boundaries of our human experience, I believe that we will see that our life, as a whole, spans the arc of a single eternal journey, a unique and individual Cosmic Hero's Journey.

GEOMETRY OF LIFE

I think that we can get a clearer picture of this Cosmic Hero's Journey by considering the geometry of life.

Remember in school when we learned about basic concepts of geometry? We learned about the differences between a line, a ray, and a line segment. A line is infinite, with no beginning and no end. A ray too is infinite, with a beginning but no end. A line segment is finite, with both a beginning and an end. All three geometries are concepts—all three geometries have zero width, for example—and so cannot actually be drawn, only illustrated:

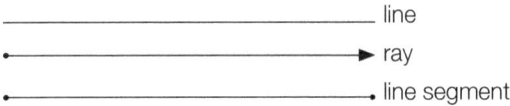

I find that the different properties of lines, line segments, and rays can help us get a handle on our world view about our lives. Some people view life as a line segment. For them, life begins at birth and ends at death. Other people view life as a ray. For them, life begins at birth and keeps going after death. I believe that life is neither a line segment nor a ray. Life is a line. Without end or beginning. You and I are eternal beings—in *both* directions: We never began, and we will never end. We are.

According to conventions of geometry, when you draw a line, you don't include arrows at the ends, as you would when you draw rays. But two connected rays that extend in opposite directions then become the same as a line, so I would diagram my concept of life this way: life extending infinitely in both directions.

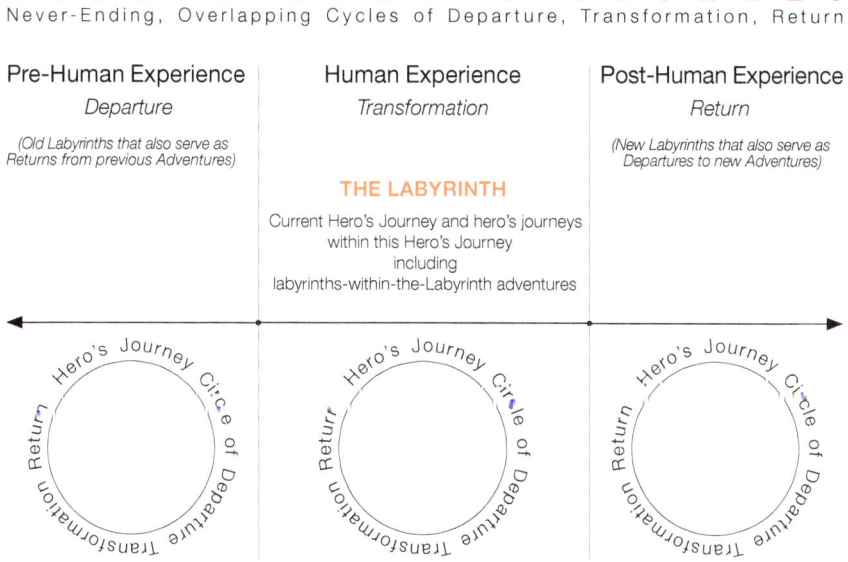

I believe that our Cosmic Lifeline includes countless line segments taking place on different planes of experience, both before and after our current, human experience. But to keep the diagram simple, I show only the line segment that represents our current, human experience.

Upshot: We are eternal spiritual beings currently having a finite human experience, and the human experience is a Labyrinth phase—a Transformation phase—in our eternal Cosmic Hero's Journey. Along this Cosmic Hero's Journey, we experience never-ending, overlapping cycles of Departure, Transformation, and Return.

Our individual Adventure is a continuously unfolding tale of creativity, bravery, perseverance, resilience, grit, skill, compassion, empathy, and enlightenment. We are on a Cosmic Hero's Journey of eternal growth and development toward a fuller understanding and expression of the art and science of life.

As my diagram shows, human experience is a Special World that we enter after our Departure from an Ordinary World of pre-human experience. But at the same time, human experience also serves as a point of Departure for our next plane of existence (our subsequent Special World), which in turn represents our Return—but only metaphorically, because I believe that rather than returning to the plane of our pre-human experience, we will wake up in an entirely new Special World that we have never seen before, some other plane of existence that becomes simultaneously our new Labyrinth phase and point of departure for our next Labyrinth phase.

For an example of this special type of Return, a Return by the hero not literally to the previous Ordinary World, but figuratively to a new Special World, we can turn once again to Daedalus.

DAEDALUS'S RETURN

"Heroes gather up what they have learned, gained, stolen, or been granted in the Special World," Vogler writes on page 200 of *The Writer's Journey*. "They set themselves a new goal, to escape, find further adventure, or return home."

We see this theme played out vividly in the life of mythical Daedalus, who set himself the goal of escaping from the Special World of Crete, which held him captive in the Labyrinth tower. And he did escape. But did he then seek further adventure or return home?

The Greek myth tells the story of Daedalus's Departure from his Ordinary World of Athens and his Transformation in the Special World of Crete, the Labyrinth phase of his Adventure—symbolized by his encounter with a physical labyrinth, in which he played multiples roles, including designer, builder, and prisoner. But the story ends with his escape from Crete and the death of his son, cutting short Daedalus's Return.

Daedalus's plight follows the classic patterns and stages of the Hero's Journey, but with a twist. The tower within the labyrinth in which Daedalus was imprisoned was his Inmost Cave, the scene of his Ordeal. And by Seizing the Sword of resilience, courage, and ingenuity, Daedalus gains the Reward of freedom for himself and Icarus. But the tragic Road Back for Daedalus will require a Resurrection. The death of Icarus, which represents the death of an extension of Daedalus's self, requires of Daedalus a resurrection of the heart. For only then could he possibly live again and keep going.

And surely Daedalus did keep going.

But again, where? Where did Daedalus fly? Home to Athens? You would think that he would be welcome there given that he had saved King Theseus's life.

Perhaps Daedalus flew to a new land. The ancient Greek storytellers leave Daedalus's destination to the flight of our imagination. But wherever he chose to go, and though his heart was heavy with grief and guilt from the loss of his son Icarus, surely the third phase of his hero's journey—Return—propelled him with newfound freedom and wisdom to brave new adventures, restarting yet again the epic cycle of his unique and never-ending Cosmic Hero's Journey.

OUR STORY

Just as Crete represents The Labyrinth phase of the Hero's Journey for Daedalus, so too for us, whatever comprises human experience is our Crete. We entered this human Labyrinth by departing from some pre-human experience, and when we exit this human Labyrinth, we will move on to some post-human experience, the next phase of our Cosmic Hero's Journey.

And when we leave our Crete, where will we go? To where will we Return? To our Athens, to the very place of our Departure? (And where is that?) Or, as I suspect, will we fly on to further adventures and create a new home?

Wherever we do end up, will we remember any more about our human experience than we currently remember about our pre-human, our pre-earthly, experience?

We know one thing for sure: While we're here, while we adventure through the Labyrinth of this Special World of human experience that provides the place for our Transformation, we have savage beasts to slay and kingdoms to save—the savage beasts of materiality, oppression, chaos, disease, error, limitation, mediocrity, vice, hate, and fear directed against the kingdoms of our health and well-being, our societies, workplaces, and homes.

We have work to do. We have the screenplay of our own Hero's Journey to write and enact. Our story has the potential to echo the story of the heroes who have gone before us—the "one shape-shifting story of the vision quest that transforms the world."[1]

And everything we need for our Adventure lies within our reach: thread, sword, and wings.

[1]"Traditionally the hero might be a warrior, the ideal of strength and courage. An explorer, a founder of civilizations. A philosopher, an adventurer of the mind. And in the modern world, Campbell would add the artist and the scientist to the pantheon of heroes, but the journey is essentially the same—one shape-shifting story of the vision quest that transforms the world."

—From the documentary *The Hero's Journey: The World of Joseph Campbell* (1987) written by Janelle Balnicke, Phil Cousineau, and William Free

Intuit and reason your way through the human Labyrinth — stay receptive to a broad spectrum of practical wisdom about the art & science of life.

Oh, and if Mind is your copilot, swap seats.

2
Suit Up

Put on the armor that protects you from monsters.

METAPHYSICAL WARRIOR

I glimpsed another secret of life when I read Nobel laureate Seamus Heaney's translation of *Beowulf*, an Old English epic composed c. 1000 CE by an anonymous poet.

Based on the oral tradition that spread the story among the Anglo-Saxons for some 400 years, *Beowulf* chronicles the adventures of the mythic Swedish hero Beowulf, who traveled to Denmark c. 400 CE and slew the monster Grendel and Grendel's monster mother.

According to Anglo-Saxon myth, all monsters descend from Cain, the Bible villain who killed his brother, Abel, out of envy and greed. So Grendel and his mother spring from the Cain family tree.

Till the end of time, monsters will roam the earth, re-enacting the Cain legacy—seeking revenge for getting dealt some bum cards.

How do we monster-proof ourselves against envy, greed, and revenge? Against double-talk, deceit, fog, force, and fraud? Against despair and hate? How do we fend off inner and outer monsters that try to ruin us? (Including monsters that coax us to punish other people.)

I crafted a prayer. Seizing the thought-sword and thought-shield of metaphysics, I welded Eddy's assurance that we are "covered from the devourer by divine protection and affection" (*Miscellaneous Writings 1883-1896*, p. 263) to what I learned from Greek myth about the Minotaur and from *Beowulf* about monsters, and I asserted, as I assert now every day:

> I am covered from the monsters of envy, greed, and revenge by divine protection and affection. Clad in the MONSTER-Proof Armor of Principle and Love, I stand undaunted and safe—shielded from the Minotaur-devourer of misery, mayhem, manipulation, and malice. What goes for me goes for everyone.
>
> That's the truth. And I expect proof.

MONSTER-Proof Armor (MPA)?

It gets sprayed with a special protective coating at the factory (a coating that can ultimately repel and break the spell of any monster).

M : Malice
O : Oblivion
N : Nonsense
S : Sabotage
T : Treachery
E : Envy
R : Revenge

Sure, some monster might land a few blows, bamboozle me, and even knock me flat. Challenge after challenge lies in wait along the hero-path through the Labyrinth of life. Because that's how life works.

Like football players in shoulder pads and helmets, we will get tackled. Even hobbled and carried to the sideline for special treatment and an equipment check. Reaching the end zone will require strength. And the higher the stakes, the tougher the Resistance (which Steven Pressfield capitalizes in *The War of Art* to highlight the universal, impersonal nature of Resistance). That's the name of the game.

So when I get conked by a monster, I remember who I am: a warmhearted, good-hearted, and brave-hearted emissary of Mind. A metaphysical warrior. A true-blue student at adversity university.

And I suit up.

I shine up my MPA. I double down on Life. And I fight back.

I remind myself that whatever monster-adversity I face boils down to a character test: a test of heart. And I pray that I will never sacrifice my character on the altar of fear and self-interest. Because that isn't what heroes do. I trust with all my heart in the MONSTER-Proof Armor of Principle and Love.

I hear The Voice promise, "I will rescue you and help you. I will safeguard and guide you. I will walk you through this challenge. I will not betray you. Nothing can stop your progress toward the realization of the worthy ideals that I have inspired in you, because I fuel your determination, integrity, and grit. I supply your opportunity and work. I shape your life. I infuse it with prosperity, mercy, and grace. Well-being, resilience, unity, and joy. Intuition, foresight, and heart. Love. And I will coach you through the labyrinth of this adversity to victory."

If you listen, you will hear the same promise.

**I coexist with and express Truth
as a sunbeam coexists with and expresses the sun.
And so do you.**

3 Illusions

Don't be manipulated by appearances.

The Red Sox were on the road in the spring of 2009 when I first ducked into the Bleacher Bar, a hole-in-the-wall joint in Fenway Park, only a fly ball away from my former apartment in the Back Bay. And when I say "in Fenway Park," I mean literally, because the Bleacher Bar hides out in the base of the left-center field wall, next to the Green Monster, the popular nickname for Fenway's thirty-seven foot high left field wall. "See Inside Fenway All Year," says the sign on the Bleacher Bar's Landsdowne Place door (you can't get in from inside Fenway). I went in because I saw from the sidewalk that the restaurant had a field-level window to the entire ball park, offering a view that stretched clear across the emerald outfield to home plate. I couldn't believe it. Wow! From the closet-like dark space of the Bleacher bar, I gazed out to the vast sun-drenched space on the other side of the outfield wall and marvelled at the prospect of watching a game from that magical secret spot.

    I went back to the Bleacher Bar when the Sox were in town. I didn't stay long, just long enough to realize that the Bleacher Bar's unusual setup on game day gave me a new insight, a memorable lesson about illusions, how they weave through the fabric of our lives in all kinds of ways that we don't see until we wake up and look.

    Gazing through the garage-door-size window, I watched a couple of pitches to Red Sox slugger David Ortiz. Then I turned to check out the bank of flat-screen TVs in the bar, broadcasting the game, and as I eye-jockeyed back and forth from the live action to the TVs, I noticed that action on the field and the action shown on the TV were out of sync, by quite a lot. I watched the pitcher go into his wind up and fire the ball toward the plate, saw Ortiz take a rip and the catcher throw the ball back to the pitcher, and then I looked over to the TV. The pitcher hadn't yet started his windup!

    Now I'd heard of the seven-second delay that broadcasters use during live events. But until that day at the Bleacher Bar, I'd never seen how the delay works firsthand. What an eye-opener. Seven seconds is a long time! A seven-second delay means all the sports action you're watching on TV is very definitely in the past. And that means that if you're a fan, and you're rooting for your team to do something dramatic, say for Ortiz to homer (or for the Celtic's Paul Pierce to nail a three-pointer at the buzzer), you're rooting in vain. You just didn't know it. *Aha*, I thought,

My perceptions and emotions are being manipulated by an illusion.

And so now I have a completely different perspective as I watch sports on TV, knowing as I do that what I'm watching has already happened, making the tension and apprehension I feel entirely bogus. We root and hope because we think that all our rooting and hoping is going on *before* the action happens. Makes sense if you're at the game, but not if you watch on TV, because we're watching a recording of what's already happened. Which means that rather than responding rationally to the way things really are, we're being manipulated by the appearance of things. And that's never a good idea. Leads to all kinds of stupid things. Like rooting for David Ortiz to crush the ball over the Green Monster on the next pitch when in fact the next pitch has already been thrown, and Ortiz whiffed.

Yes, despite appearances, the moon has no light of its own, the sun doesn't rise or set, matter isn't nearly as solid as it appears, and as I now know, live baseball games that you watch on TV are not live, but took place seven seconds ago.

The moral of the story? Human life presents a labyrinth of illusions, and zapping these illusions leads to wisdom, progress, and health, sparing us the emotional and physical effects of being fooled and manipulated by false appearances. Because bottom line: Manipulation by false appearances makes us afraid. As somebody once said: FEAR = **F**alse **E**vidence **A**ppearing **R**eal. And as I recently saw written on the whiteboard of Sunday School in Quincy, Massachusetts: FEAR = **F**orgetting **E**verything **A**bout **R**eality.

Yet as Mary Baker Eddy recognized, Jesus wasn't fooled by False Evidence Appearing Real. He didn't Forget Everything About Reality. Jesus wasn't afraid. As I point out in my *Christian Science Sentinel* editorial, "F.E.A.R.," October 25, 2010, through reliance on Spirit, Jesus was able to **F**ace **E**very **A**dversity **R**ighteously.

Jesus healed through right thinking—through fearless dominion empowered by an illusion-free view of Reality. He healed by a metaphysical process, in which he saw that all inharmony of the body or experience is an illusion and the remedy is Truth—the deep, spiritual Truth that disease, discord, and other forms of misery ultimately have no reality, and therefore no power.

Even those who have not fully seen, as Eddy saw, that matter itself is an illusion have glimpsed that illusions riddle mortal life. Albert Einstein warned of the traps sprung by "an optical illusion of consciousness." In *A New Earth* (p. 250), Eckhart Tolle summed up that "the physical body is no more than a misperception of who you are."

Joseph Campbell saw that we can emerge from the maze of illusions and misperceptions (the misadventures!) of human life as heroes, overcoming adversity, sidestepping land mines, and safely journeying through inner and outer transformation by virtue of innate spiritual gifts such as fortitude and prudence.

And I've learned this: When we go up to the plate with the Louisville Slugger baseball bat of truth—a home-run hitter's illusion-free, *scientific metaphysical perspective*—our lives get better. We undergo improvement and progress. This outlook can guide anyone along their inner quest and outer quest, instilling in us the spiritually-fueled power, patience, endurance, courage, calm, and presence of Mind to do what Eddy said we could do: "Meet every adverse circumstance as its master."

Thereby rocketing our lives into the light . . . up and over the Green Monster.

So let's Face Every Adversity Righteously as a Metaphysical Warrior. Then watch as illusions dissolve and dilemmas resolve.

And get a grip as you watch the Red Sox on TV battle when they're down to their last strike in the bottom of the ninth. Don't buy the illusion. The game's already over. (They won.)

> **You don't see your prison because its bars are invisible.**
> —Dan Millman

Do not allow yourself to be misled by the surfaces of things.
—Rainer Maria Rilke

The Bleacher Bar, Fenway Park.

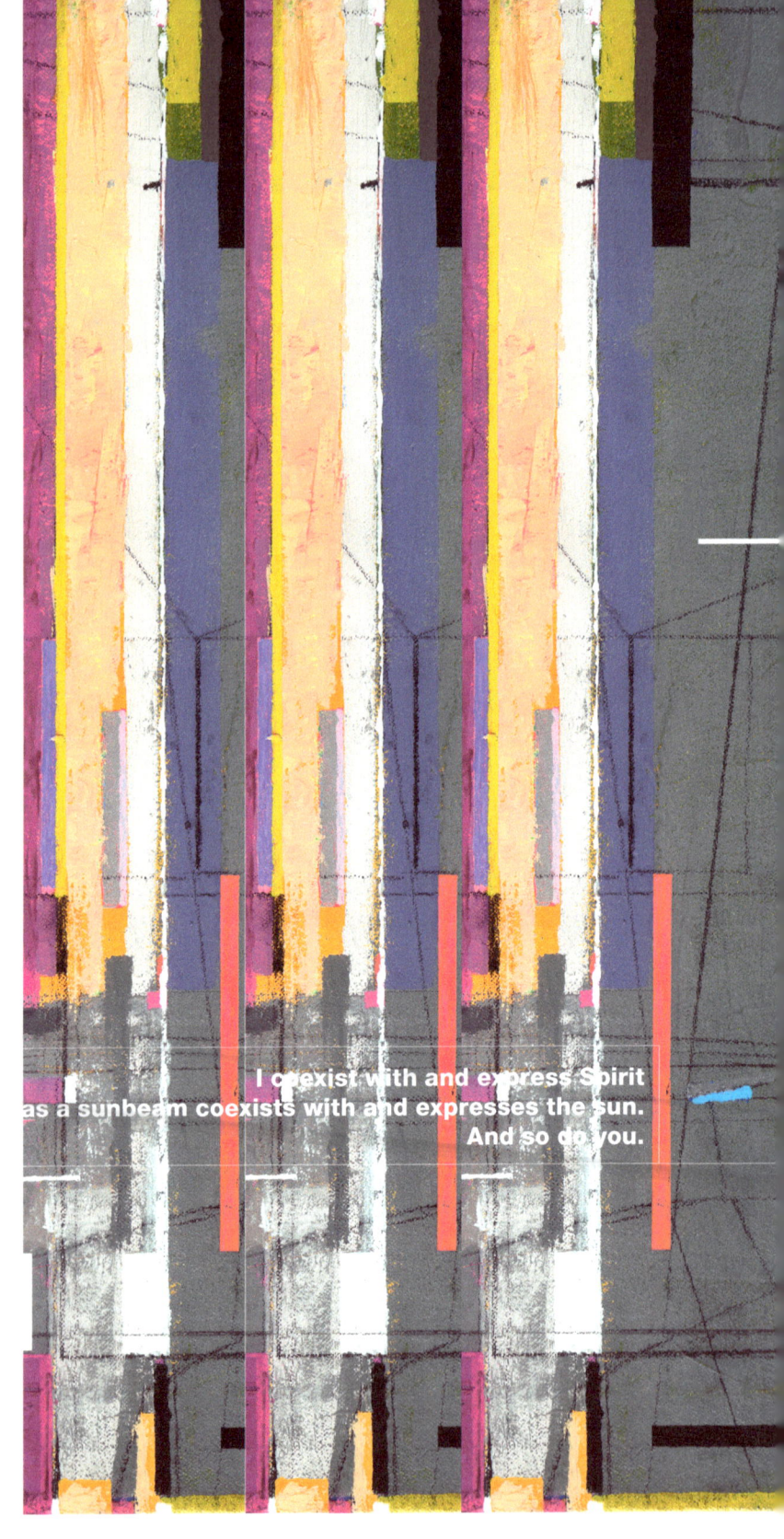

4
Opportunity Will Find You

Who knows what favorable circumstances await along life's highway.

Your car's headlamps can cut through the night—but not enough to light up the entire journey. Still, do you worry? No. You know the road doesn't end. Even though you can't see beyond a hundred feet or so, you know you'll be OK. So you drive on, trusting you'll see what you need to safely navigate the road ahead.

You can choose to drive through life the same way.

Especially since Good—another name for God, the one Mind and Soul—beams a deep, eternal, cosmic GPS that can guide and safeguard you.

So flip the switch. Turn on your spiritual GPS. Feel fear lift. Sit back and let Good steer you.

You'll experience insights and soul-moments that awaken in you the wisdom and strength—the resilience—you need to keep moving forward. You'll see breathtaking vistas that summon in you creativity, special talents, and purpose. And Good will never let you get lost. Good will course-correct you. So trust Good to cruise-control you safely through a unique and meaningful and rewarding life-adventure.

That's what I've learned.

And I've also learned this: As you motor along life's unpredictable highways and byways toward your destiny—opportunity will find you.

You may even find yourself on an odyssey, doubling back to where you began, to a home where you were once unwelcome, bringing new wisdom and strength and transformation to a place you least expect.

Life works this way. And at the same time, as Dan Eldon famously put it in his journals: "The journey is the destination."

So enjoy the ride! Fearless. Confident. Humble. Bold. Alive! Forever-enriching yourself through education, dedication, and expectation.

And give to others along the way. Give generously. Because if you have glimpsed these truths, then you have everything you could ever need to adventure through life with enthusiasm and hope. You will surely find what Dan Millman calls "unreasonable happiness" ("be happy *now*, for no reason")—not simply happiness that the circumstances justify or happiness that you think you deserve or ought reasonably to have, but happiness *now!*—and happiness *beyond all reason!*

So give. Spiritually speaking, you already have all—just as the number 37 already has all it requires: There's nothing missing from its identity, and no way it could ever be diminished or weakened, no matter how many times people use it! So, too, you will not be depleted by giving, but enriched! And the spiritual-boomerang effect assures that the generosity of blessings you radiate to others will return to you in abundance beyond measure.

Including opportunity. For opportunity will find you.

Because on the highway of life, opportunity is a magnet, pulling you along to the road-side diner of wisdom or the mountain-top lodges of insight or the industrial parks of innovation you need for your trip. Opportunity, like some god, knows what makes you tick.

Which brings us to one of life's many secrets: The opportunity you seek, seeks you. And that's why—

Opportunity will find you.

And knowing that, affirming that, is in itself a prayer.

So let's expect our prayer to work. Expect our solid metaphysical understanding that Good flows continuously through our lives, bringing us rich and rewarding opportunities—expect this reasoning to produce tangible results.

The same Life that *inspires* good ideas and rational perspectives *unleashes* the full potential of these ideas and perspectives, nourishing them to fruition, giving us solid proof of the practical effect of seeing and affirming the truth about Life.

And so my prayer, another thought-sword anthem of the metaphysical warrior:

> Here, now, this moment and eternally, I abound in good beyond measure—good in every form, including opportunity, skill, serenity, wealth, and health—because Life, which I coexist with and express as a sunbeam coexists with and expresses the sun, abounds in good beyond measure. What goes for me goes for everyone.
>
> That's the truth. And I expect proof.

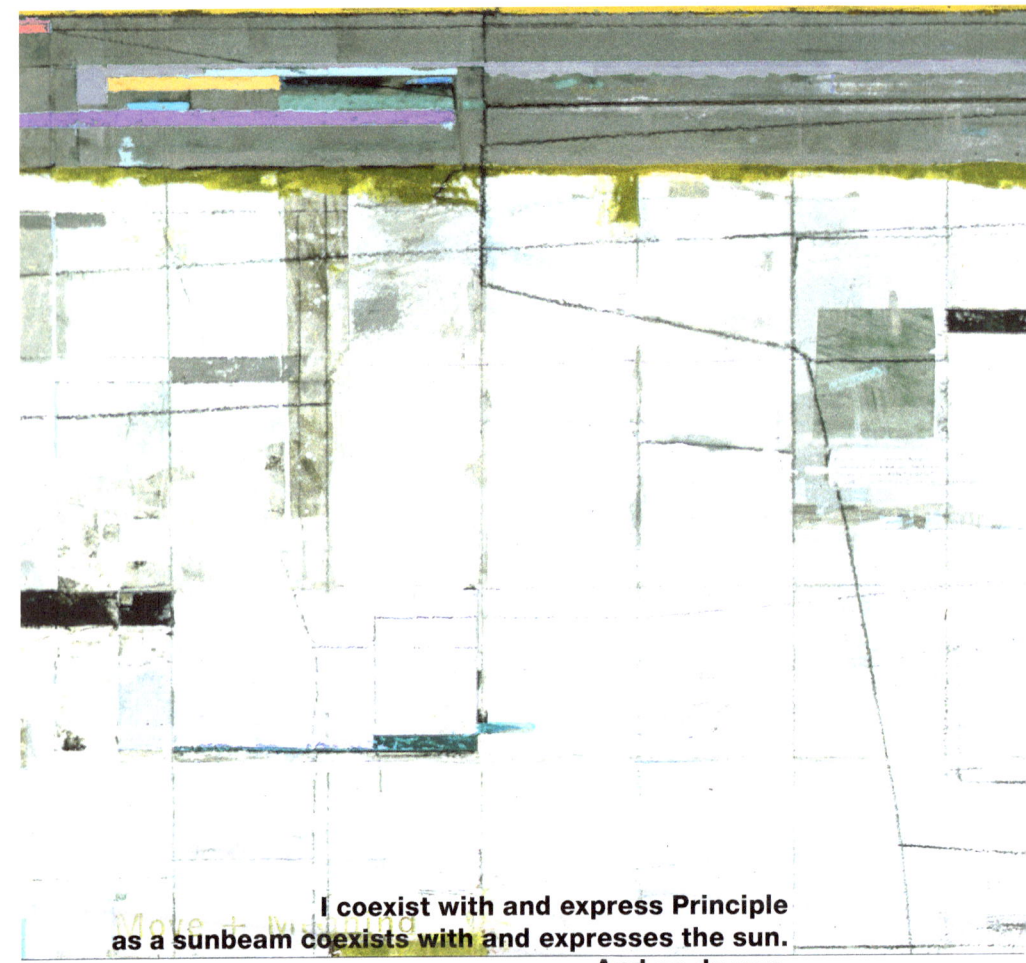

5
The Scientific Way

Grasp the truth. Expect proof.

"MEET EVERY ADVERSE CIRCUMSTANCE AS ITS MASTER"—
How do you do that?

I asked myself that question as I sat bundled up in a parka and blankets on the ninth floor balcony of a hotel in Ocean City, Maryland, during a freezing, black February morning in 2009 at 4:30 a.m., an hour before first light.

Now for some time before that morning, I'd taken up the challenge of that seven-word imperative, which Mary Baker Eddy spelled out in *Science and Health* (p. 419). I'd adopted the line as a kind of anthem, or slogan, seeking to live my life on those terms. I liked the compact, streamlined construction of Eddy's sentence—and how it reverberates with self-empowerment. I liked its simple, yet deep heroic message, a message free from religious jargon. And it stuck.

So the line had been rattling around in my head for a while. You might say it was the background wallpaper on the computer screen of my life! But it leaped to the foreground that winter morning in the form of a question because for some time I'd been pondering the answer.

You see, I knew the answer, at least my answer. The answer that worked for me. But I hadn't yet peeled back the layers of that answer. And that's what I began to do that morning.

Let me take you on my thought-journey during that hour before dawn. And I'll start with the punch line, so you know where we're headed. How do you "Meet every adverse circumstance as its master"?

The scientific way.

And the scientific way means this:

Grasp the truth.

Then expect proof.

LIGHT BENDS

This simple principle of the scientific way—grasp the truth then expect proof—really hit home when I learned the story of Albert Einstein and his General Theory of Relativity.

Einstein powered his physics research by the twin engines of the scientific method: conjecture and observation. For Einstein, conjecture was math-based, and once he did the math—once he saw that his conjecture must be true—*he expected proof.*

Einstein published his astonishing Special Theory of Relativity in 1905. That theory included his famous equation, $E=mc^2$. But in 1911, Einstein completed four frustrating years struggling to perfect his General Theory of Relativity, in which he solved the mystery of gravity. Gravity happens, Einstein discovered, because space curves. And because space curves and gravity therefore acts on all things, light bends.

Einstein grasped this startling truth, but now he needed vivid proof. He knew that the radical concepts at the heart of his General Theory wouldn't be accepted until he could demonstrate them. Because as Andrea Ghez, Professor of Astronomy at UCLA puts it, "If it's not a testable hypothesis, it's not science, it's science fiction."

So Einstein asked himself, Where would gravity be strong enough to bend light enough to observe it? And it hit him: the sun. He postulated that during a total solar eclipse of the sun the sky would be dark enough to see the positions of stars in the field of view of the sun and observe that light bends. So he published his revolutionary prediction in 1915 and called on astronomers to do the eclipse test.

Enter British astronomer Arthur Eddington. The beautiful movie *Einstein and Eddington* portrays Eddington's expedition to the island of Principe (off the west coast of Africa), where he took photographs during the solar eclipse of May 29, 1919. Sure enough, the photographs confirmed Einstein's theory of gravity.

And here's the kicker, another principle of science that I seek to apply in my work as a metaphysicist. Here's what Einstein revealed about his state of mind on the eve of that solar eclipse when his grand theory hung in the balance. Speaking about renowned physicist Max Planck, who helped him with the math, Einstein said, "He was one of the finest people I have ever known . . . but he didn't really understand physics, [because] during the eclipse of 1919 he stayed up all night to see if it would confirm the bending of light by the gravitational field. If he had really understood [the general theory of relativity], he would have gone to bed the way I did."

How do people who really understand science behave during the gap between the discernment of truth and proof of that truth? No worries. With absolute fear-free confidence. Total doubt-free anticipation. Calm certainty. Peace.

EARTH SPINS

Which brings us back to that cold Atlantic coast morning in 2009. As I waited for first light there on that oceanfront balcony, I asked myself what I was waiting for. And I thought, *the sunrise*.

And then my wheels began turning, first toward one insight, then toward an even bigger insight. *But the sun doesn't rise*, I thought, proceeding along these lines: Sunrise is a figure of speech. It describes an illusion, a misperception, an unscientific assumption. It's a pretty evocation built on a false premise. But the trope endures, I told myself, because of its uplifting poetic value, and therefore its inspiring symbolic, spiritual value. Greeting the sunrise means greeting the rise in consciousness of the inspiration, reassurance, and comfort that pours in to reinvigorate and fortify us for that day and for our lifetime ahead. And I loved that meaning. I didn't want to give it up. Why should I? After all, I knew that I wasn't fooled by the concept of sunrise, as I had just verified yet again to myself by the above analysis. But I kept going, asking myself to replace the poetic but false notion of what I was waiting for on that cold, dark morning as I looked toward the faint blurry line where ocean and sky meet at the horizon, nudging myself to replace that primitive notion of sunrise with the truth. And that's when things started falling into place.

I pictured what really was happening, scientifically, according to the truth about the earth's relationship to the sun. I pictured myself hurtling toward the sun at 1,000 miles per hour on the surface of a giant sphere that was tilted off vertical axis away from the sun because it was winter in the northern hemisphere. I factored in that in addition to this motion of the earth's daily rotation around its axis, I was also moving at some unknown speed around the sun in a path of yearly revolution. Plus the sun and earth were moving together through the ocean of galaxies in another motion path and at another speed. And I felt the thrill of recognition as I tried to visualize my ride on the back of Planet Earth through this three-layered motion matrix. And I felt the soft thrill of the ride itself. Suddenly I no longer felt I was sitting still on that balcony waiting for something to happen on a motionless earth. Suddenly I was moving. The earth was moving. We were spinning toward the sun, and I was waiting for the first glimpse of solar light as the world turned.

All during this thought experiment I was also picturing myself from space, viewing myself as a dot on the northern hemisphere of earth, viewing the relationship of the earth to the sun and their place in the Milky Way galaxy and the Milky Way's place in the whole shebang. I couldn't get a handle on the last part—my understanding of the Milky Way's position in the cosmic cauldron of stars and space was, yes, milky. And to get a handle on the first part, I had to set up in my mind those models of the earth and sun we used in 5th-grade science class to show how the earth rotates and revolves relative to the sun. I transposed these models in my head to my external reality, and I began to see these solar system partners, earth and sun, in real time. Right where I was. And I was part of it. An extra, perhaps. But connected. In the mix. And here's the cool thing: The more clearly I began to see and feel what was actually happening to me right that second right there on that balcony, the less the notion of sunrise seemed quite so poetic and necessary any more. It began to lose its hold on me. The scientific model was bumping "sunrise" aside. In fact, this model collided with all perceptions and inverted them. Here was the ocean rolling in onto the shore toward me, but I saw that the ocean and I were actually moving together in the opposite direction—spinning in the direction of the horizon line, backwards relative to the ocean's forward motion toward me! Suddenly everything seemed paradoxical, the opposite of how things had appeared only minutes earlier when I saw myself as sitting still and the ocean and the sun moving toward me. I now saw that in truth I was in motion, moving with the ocean toward the sun in the opposite direction from the ocean's wave-breaking direction on the shore below me. I had somersaulted my way beyond a series of illusions to see that things were not at all the way they seemed. I was earthspinning toward the sun. That was the scientific truth. And I knew I would soon see proof. Sunlight.

MISPLACED METAPHORS

During that morning hour, before the darkness gave way to morning light, picturing and feeling myself earthspinning to sunlight, I also examined favorite Bible verses. (Yes, I was intense!) I asked myself to what degree the metaphorical language of the Bible might be obstructing my grasp of scientific clarity. I recalled the 91st Psalm, verses 10 and 11:

"There shall no evil befall thee, neither shall any plague come nigh thy dwelling. For he shall give his angels charge over thee, to keep thee in all thy ways." Scientific translation: Divine Mind gives pure and perfect spiritual intuitions charge over me. They control me, my thinking, and therefore my experience. But what's this about "angels," which evokes images of spiritual beings with wings (and requires that I "translate")? And what's this use of "he" to refer to God, which I know to be Truth! And Life, Mind, Soul, and Spirit!

So I came to this conclusion: Poetic imagery and metaphorical language, as much as these move me and I love them, can cloud scientific clarity. And therefore can cloud a clear view of truth. And therefore can obstruct the scientific way. And without the scientific way, we are lost. Rambling around in a poetically infused but nonetheless dark night of mortality, trapped unwittingly in a labyrinth of misperceptions that keep us from seeing and experiencing the escape we hope for. "To begin rightly is to end rightly," declared Eddy, articulating the axiom to which all scientists ascribe. We can only end with the scientific proof we hope for if we begin with an unambiguous conception of what is truly scientific. Which means, as I forced myself to do that morning, pushing aside metaphorical and poetic interference, however beloved, and getting rigorously scientific about what we acknowledge and affirm—and therefore expect.

Now I haven't given up poetic language. I'm a sucker for it. And I'm still inner wrestling with my deep-seated notion that the poetic and metaphorical represent integral and valid dimensions of life and help us to unlock, behold, and appreciate life's true setup. But I'm wary. I won't let nostalgic poetic language and misplaced metaphors distract me from the truth that I so desperately need to discern clearly if I'm to experience the healing, dominion, and good I yearn for.

Metaphorical language and poetic imagery, such as referring to the sunrise and sunset, or referring to God anthropomorphically—calling God He or She, Father or Mother, and thinking of oneself as resting in the palm of His hand—can inspire and comfort. I know the warm and fuzzy and very real, healing influence those ways of thinking about God can have, especially when sustained by a correct view of God. And I'm not making a case for a cold way of thinking about God, simply an accurate way, which turns out to be equally warm and fuzzy! I'm simply saying that words like "angels" and "He" carry a lot of baggage, unscientific baggage, and clinging to these ways of embracing reality can come with a price. Illusions can be tough to cut through. And outdated words and imagery can keep those illusions going, illusions that unwittingly undercut your effort to escape suffering. The prison-house of inherited words, metaphors, and concepts can keep us mired in a false view of reality and therefore keep us from seeing the truth that will set us free.

SCIENTIFIC CONSCIOUSNESS

Einstein came up with a great phrase to explain what he saw as the illusion that humans are somehow separate from one another. He said that misperception arises from an "optical illusion of consciousness."

Great line. And a perfect description of what Eddy cut through, discovering that mortal life isn't what it's cracked up to be, illuminating the scientific truth of our immortal being. In fact, on page 121 of *Science and Health*, Eddy used the very metaphor of the earth's rotation to get at how truth sweeps away misperceptions that handcuff us: "The earth's diurnal rotation is invisible to the physical eye, and the sun seems to move from east to west, instead of the earth from west to east. Until rebuked by clearer views of the everlasting facts, this false testimony of the eye deluded the judgment and induced false conclusions."

And a perfect description, as well, of what I cut through that Atlantic-ocean earthspin day. I haven't seen life the same way since. Having traded in the "optical illusion of consciousness" of "sunrise" for the truth of "earthspin," having challenged my reliance on misleading poetic imagery and metaphors to describe my relationship to divine Being, I applied my new-found insight into the scientific method (affirm truth then expect proof) to my life.

Let me give you a couple of examples of how I pray the scientific way, inspired by what I saw that special morning, building on what I've learned from my lifelong study of Christian Science.

Truth: Here, now, this moment and eternally I abound in good beyond measure because Life, which I coexist with and represent (as a sunbeam coexists with and represents the sun), abounds in good beyond measure. I affirm this truth and expect to see proof.

Truth: Here, now, this moment and eternally, I radiate abundance beyond measure because Soul, with which I coexist and express (like a sunbeam coexists with and expresses the sun), radiates abundance beyond measure. That's the truth, and I expect proof. Which means that abundance doesn't exist "out there," outside of me. I am the very expression of abundance. I radiate abundance! Opportunity, creativity, productivity, ample provisions and supplies to fully realize creativity and productivity—these are not things I have to get. These are things I already include. They comprise my essence, my substance, identity. As integral to who I am as warmth and beauty and vitality are to a sunbeam. That's the truth, and I expect proof.

Truth: Here, now, this moment and eternally, I am immortal, incorporeal, exempt from aging, decaying, disease, and death, because Life, which I coexist with and represent (as a sunbeam coexists with and represents the sun), is immortal, incorporeal, exempt from aging, decaying, disease, and death. That's the truth, and I expect proof.

And when it comes to scientifically nixing the false belief of age and deterioration, as well as affirming the continuous flow of opportunity, skill, and fruition in life, I've found additional import in the analogy of a sunbeam, whose radiance and reach cannot wane. Thus my daily prayer: Here, now, this moment and eternally, nothing can dull, diminish, or darken my radiance and reach, because nothing can dull, diminish, or darken the radiance and reach of Life, with which I coexist and express—any more than the radiance and reach of a sunbeam, which coexists with and expresses the sun, can dull, diminish, or darken. That's the truth, and I expect proof.

The scientific way of praying means this: affirming the truth about Life (God, the source of our being) and expecting this truth to play itself out in human experience in good, powerful, and even astonishing ways. And the basis for this expectation? Certainty that Life rests on a Principle and that we can count on this Life-Principle to trump any trouble, dissolve any discord, and make everything right.

META-CARE

Eddy uses the phrase "scientific truth" several times in her published writings, and she uses the phrase "scientific way" once, in a paragraph in which she differentiates between healing physical maladies through "arguments of truth" versus healing instantaneously: "If Spirit or the power of divine Love bear witness to the truth, this is the ultimatum, the scientific way, and the healing is instantaneous" (*Science and Health*, p. 411). That's where I got the phrase "the scientific way." I remember reading that sentence one day, some time before my Atlantic ocean epiphany, and those three words jumped off the page: *the scientific way.*

And they've stayed with me.

And so has Eddy's assertion that the scientific way has the power to heal the physical body, as her sentence above says. The adverse circumstances of our bodies can be corrected by meeting those circumstances as their master. Eddy indicates how in this line (*Science and Health*, p. 369): "In proportion as matter loses to human sense all entity as man, in that proportion does man become its master."

I've been healed of various illnesses throughout my life by embracing this principle. It's a sound, metaphysical principle that has a practical, health-giving effect on one's physical body. Physical scientists have found that matter isn't the solid substance it appears to be. And lots of thought-explorers today are catching a glimpse that our true being is entirely separate from matter, which, as Eddy figured out, adds up to no more than an illusion. I like the way New Age author Eckhart Tolle puts it: "The physical body is no more than a misperception of who you are." And that realization—a truly scientific realization—forms part of the basis for why you can master the physical body *metaphysically*! Because anyone can master a misperception. You change your mind. You get the right picture. You wipe off the mist and grime from your lens on life and see yourself as you really are: 100% spiritual. And on that basis, empowered by your correct, scientific perspective, you can with authority say NO to the powerless illusion of illness and YES to the powerful reality of health and wholeness in form and function.

So when I face physical trouble, I don't turn to matter for rescue and freedom. I turn for help to the same power that I turn to when I face other kinds of trouble: Spirit. I rely on the dynamic health-sustaining laws of divine Principle, Love. I rely on Truth to set me free. I rely on Mind's provision of what I term "**Meta-care**."

Meta-care is Spirit-sourced health care—offering round-the-clock coverage to any metaphysical warrior who yields to its provisions and power. I feel a deep peace, a sure sense that I am safe and sound, when I remind myself that I am spiritual, the very expression and essence of Spirit, and so every aspect of my experience and being is at all times ordered and sustained by Spirit.

I've learned to trust divine Meta-care to meet my every human need and guarantee my well-being, including "financial peace" (money expert Dave Ramsey's beautiful term), creativity, work, intuition, mercy, love, and physical health.

In the same way that a sunbeam is the physical radiance of the sun, we are the spiritual radiance of Mind. Our consciousness, identity, and well-being emanate from Mind. So we can no more be cut off from Mind or Spirit than a star beam can be cut off from a star.

I am the divine starlight. And so are you.

Many people have glimpsed this truth—listen to Andrew Lloyd Webber and Richard Stilgoe's song "I Am The Starlight" from their musical *Starlight Express*. And as we get in touch with our true starlight-like identity—inseparable from Spirit and Mind—we can begin to see through the illusion of matter. We start to feel confident that our body isn't what it seems. It isn't physical. It's mental—a mental projection of the human mind. Our human body and experience are a feature film produced by human consciousness. And when we grasp this and see ourselves as the emanation of Spirit, our human consciousness improves, which naturally leads to an improved human body and experience. By exchanging a counterfeit consciousness based on the illusion of matter for true Consciousness based on the reality of Mind, we can expect the movie-quality of our lives to upgrade from home-movie 2-D to IMAX 3-D.

As Mary Baker Eddy explained (*Science and Health*, p. 425), "Consciousness constructs a better body when faith in matter has been conquered. Correct material belief by spiritual understanding, and Spirit will form you anew."

SEAL THE DEAL

To the degree that we get a read on life's setup and *grasp the truth*—understand it and seize it—our quality of life will go up.

But don't forget to seal the deal: *Expect proof.*

Life is a science project. We work in the laboratory of thought, and you can choose right this moment to assert the truth and expect proof.

I apply this scientific approach to the lower-ladder stuff of day-to-day living as well as to my higher quest for purpose, fruition, and happiness, and I've seen good flow into my life, including new opportunities, creative freedom, companionship, financial peace, and well-being.

Everyone can follow the scientific way. Everyone can discover its practical power. Starting today, you can shape your life around the one-two-punch of the Eddy-principle "**Meet every adverse circumstance as its master**" (*every* adverse circumstance) and the Einstein-principle—the basic principle of science and so just as much the Eddy-principle as the Einstein-principle: **Grasp the truth. Then expect proof.**

Grasping truth has a powerful, practical impact on our lives. As Jesus assured (John 8:32): "And ye shall know the truth, and the truth shall make you free."

You can deeply, earnestly—and peacefully—affirm what you know is true: Your substance, your wholeness, happiness, and freedom, spring not from matter but from Spirit. You can affirm that you are therefore already as fully formed and functional, as truly ideal and conceptual, perfect and whole, as the number 9. And you can cry with all the authority that springs from the infinite depths of the spiritual universe that sustains and maintains you: *That's the truth. And I expect proof!*

In fact, due to the elastic, Mobius-strip continuum of time—and the solid metaphysical nature of reality—we can start with the end in mind and say thank you in advance: *Thanks for the proof.*

Thanks, O Life, which I coexist with and represent (as a sunbeam coexists with and represents the sun) for your astonishing and steady scientific action and power! Right now. Right here. This moment. Thanks, O Mind, for assuring me:

The science is sound.

So expect proof . . . to abound.

6
Flight 1866

Purpose and fulfillment begin with "why."

PEOPLE DON'T BUY WHAT YOU DO, THEY BUY WHY YOU DO IT.
—Simon Sinek

My former father-in-law, Fred, worked for TWA, which started in 1925 and merged with American Airlines in 2001. Fred worked as a member of the ground crew. He headed up the graveyard shift, working through the night and returning to his family at dawn. Fred did this for some 30 years before retiring. He was dedicated and true blue. So if you flew TWA, you could rest assured that the maintenance of your plane was OK. The conscientious and skilled TWA ground crew conducted aircraft diagnostics and repairs as if members of their own families were on board.

But ask Fred what TWA was all about, and never for a second would it flash through his mind that TWA was in the airplane maintenance business. Like every employee (and customer), Fred knew that TWA's healthy-airplane program played a supporting role to TWA's true business: flying.

And the people who ran TWA knew something else crucial to the success of their business: Flying adds up to a lot more than the practical function of safely transporting people from point A to point B. Check out some of TWA's vintage ads:

- **Dreams span the seas sometimes** (1953)
- **Dad's favorite chair** (1951)
- **Free as the birds** (1945)

TWA was in the business of fulfilling dreams, providing comfort and rest, and bringing people freedom.

As airlines continue to do every day, TWA carried passengers beyond their ordinary boundaries of space and time and tapped into people's innate sense of adventure and wonder, giving fliers new and breathtaking views of the world that we can't get from our routine earthbound perspective.

Through the "miracle" of flight, TWA enabled people to soar.

Which brings me to this . . .

STARTING POINTS

In the fall of 2010, a buddy at work sent me a link to a YouTube video of Simon Sinek's 2009 TED talk, "How great leaders inspire action," based on his book, *Start With Why*. Watch it. It's worth it. Sinek might get your wheels turning too.

(Don't let the brief segment about the brain keep you from sifting the chaff from the wheat and homing in on the core insights from beginning to end.)

Sinek calls himself a "buyologist," someone who studies what makes humans tick when it comes to buying things. Sinek probes the art and science of buying, mainly to help companies learn how to best reach their target audience and prosper, how to create a win-win for companies and customers.

And here's the major takeaway: Most average or struggling companies (and people) emphasize "what." But successful companies emphasize "why." Because, as Sinek says: "People don't buy what you do, they buy *why* you do it."

Sinek gives an example. He contrasts two computer companies: Dell and Apple. Dell focuses on what. Apple focuses on why. Sinek explains:

> If Apple were like everyone else, a marketing message from them might go like this: We make great computers (the "what"). They're beautifully designed, simple to use, and user friendly (the "how"). Want to buy one?
>
> And that's how most of us communicate. That's how most marketing is done. That's how most sales is done. That's how most of us communicate interpersonally: We say what we do, we say how we're different or how we're better—and we expect some kind of behavior, a purchase or vote or something like that. But it's uninspiring.
>
> Here's how Apple actually communicates: Everything we do—we believe in challenging the status quo. We believe in thinking differently (the "why"). The way we challenge the status quo is by making our products beautiful, simple to use, and user friendly (the "how"). We just happen to make great computers (the "what").

Remember Apple's ad campaign way back? What Apple put on billboards? "Think different." Not: "We make beautiful user-friendly computers." They sold "why," not "what."

STRAIGHT TALK

I started to wonder about the organization that I worked for at the time:

The First Church of Christ, Scientist, in Boston (also known as The Mother Church), headquarters for the Christian Science Church and its worldwide branches. What does this organization emphasize? "What" or "why"?

Plus, this second question: On the "struggling, average, or successful" scale, where does the Church stand? Because maybe those two questions connect.

Let's start with question two. Answer: Struggling.

Look at the negative bottom line of The Christian Science Publishing Society, which publishes periodicals started by Christian Science founder, Mary Baker Eddy. Year after year, *The Christian Science Monitor*, for example, operates deeply in the red.

Look at the dwindling Christian Science Church membership roster and dwindling or steadily low attendance at branch church services. Even major metropolitan churches generate only low-to-mid double-digit attendance. Despite rationalizations and statements defending the status quo by some titleholders in the organization who maintain that numbers don't matter, you probably won't hear many Christian Scientists seriously maintain that dwindling membership is a welcome sign of the Church's health.

Look at the scale-back of the Church's headquarters. The employee population that once required three buildings (one of them 22 stories) now requires just one 11-story building that remains only partially filled.

Though overall the Christian Science Church remains financially solvent, Christian Science looks like a movement that's retracting rather than expanding, at least in North America.

Don't get me wrong. Never underestimate the impact that Christian Science has made on the lives of countless people around the globe since Mary Baker Eddy discovered Christian Science in 1866. It helps people like me every day.

But Mary Baker Eddy hoped to reach countless receptive hearts with the Truth that Christian Science reveals. More than 125 years ago, she wrote in *Science and Health*, "Millions of unprejudiced minds—simple seekers for Truth, weary wanderers, athirst in the desert—are waiting and watching for rest and drink. Give them a cup of cold water in Christ's name, and never fear the consequences" (p. 570). As things now stand, millions of unprejudiced minds waiting and watching for that cup of cold water go thirsty, because despite the Church's best efforts, Christian Science fails to reach these weary wanderers.

Why? Could there be a link between the Church's struggling status and its emphasis on "what" rather than "why"?

I wouldn't rule it out. And Sinek's research holds out the promise that changing the focus to "why" could bring about a turnaround.

In his TED talk, Sinek describes what he calls "the golden circle": three concentric circles of success. He puts "why" at the center; "how" in the next circle; and "what" on the outer circle. He explains that ordinary people and organizations work from the outside in: They lead with "what" then follow up with "how" and "why." But successful people and organizations work from the inside out: They lead with "why" then follow up with "how" and "what."

Seems to me that a turnaround by the Christian Science Church could require their marketing and communications staff, as well as members worldwide, to lead with "why" then follow up with "how" and "what."

Let's back up. Why do I say that the Christian Science Church currently focuses on "what," not "why"? Especially given that the Church focuses on healing. Surely healing is the "why," isn't it?

"The ancient Christians were healers. Why has this element of Christianity been lost?" wrote Eddy in *Science and Health*. Eddy's discovery of Christian Science restored the practice of Christian healing to the world, healing conducted in Christ Jesus's way spiritually, metaphysically. She stated her institutional objective in the *Church Manual* (p. 17): "To organize a church designed to commemorate the word and works of our Master [Jesus], which should reinstate primitive Christianity and its lost element of healing."

Little wonder then that the question, *What is the purpose of Christian Science*—its "why"—goes unexamined. Christian Scientists, not without reason, assume they already know the "why": *healing*.

And so you hear the frequent refrain, *We are a church of healers.*

But Eddy conveyed throughout her writings that the purpose of Christian Science, as distinguished from the purpose of the Church she established in support of Christian Science, extended beyond primitive

Christianity's lost element of healing. She wrote in *Science and Health* (p. 150), "Now, as then, signs and wonders are wrought in the metaphysical healing of physical disease; but these signs are only to demonstrate its divine origin, —to attest the reality of the higher mission of the Christ-power to take away the sins of the world."

Obviously the "higher mission" of Christian Science extends beyond healing. Add everything up, and it would be reasonable for Christian Scientists to rally around a core message that runs something like this: *We are a church of healers—through reliance on the Christ-power that Christian Science unveils, we heal people of physical illness and help rid the world of sin.*

A NEW ANGLE

But what if we looked at things from a slightly different angle. What if we considered this core message not as the "why" of Christian Science, but as the "what"?

What if healing and taking away the sins of the world are "what" Christian Science does. And "what" the Church does in the service of Christian Science. Not the "why."

For one thing, we could view this new angle as signaling great promise for an organization seeking a turnaround. The "what" remains valid, and the Christian Science Church needs to simply shift its emphasis to "why." (Whereas a turnaround could prove far more daunting for a struggling organization already emphasizing "why.")

Remember: Unsuccessful or average organizations that limp along emphasize "what." Successful, healthy, growing organizations emphasize "why." These organizations clearly spell out the "why-how-what" message—leading with "why"—and rally everyone in the organization around that message.

What if communication about Christian Science by the Church to its membership and worldwide audience—as well as communication by Christian Scientists to their neighbors—started with "why" and then moved to "how" and "what." What would that message sound like?

So that brings us to the key question: If healing physical disease and redeeming the world of sin is the "what" of Christian Science, what is the "why"?

PICTURE A BILLBOARD

My wheels started turning long before I saw Simon Sinek's TED video. For example, my ears perked up when a Christian Science teacher said the following at the Annual Meeting of The Mother Church in June 2010: "We know that everything in Christian Science is about healing."

As a lifelong student of Christian Science, to me that statement didn't ring true. I said to myself, *I don't know that everything in Christian Science is about healing—any more than I know that everything in flight science is about repairing aircraft.*

Picture a billboard. What does it say? Fill in the blank:
"Christian Science— _____ since 1866"
(the year Eddy discovered Christian Science).

- **All about healing** since 1866
- **Healing people and taking away the sins of the world** since 1866
- **Restoring the lost element of primitive Christianity** since 1866

Or:

- **Bringing people health and other blessings—freedom—** since 1866

Picture another billboard. What does it say? Fill in the blank:
"The Church of Christ, Scientist—_____since 1879"
(the year Eddy formed her Church).

- **A church of healers** since 1879

Or:

- **Helping people lean on "the sustaining infinite"** since 1879

Eddy didn't title her textbook on Christian Science, *Science and Healing*: She called it *Science and Health*. And the first line of her book tips us off to what she prized: "To those leaning on the sustaining infinite, today is big with blessings." She didn't say, "big with healing." She said, "big with blessings."

Yes, some people want healing.

But *everyone* wants health. And *everyone* wants other blessings too.

Everyone wants blessings in their personal life, as well as in their family, career, and work life, blessings such as happiness, creativity, and purpose. Opportunity, skill, and wisdom. Courage, strength, and peace. And basic human needs: clothing, food, shelter, money, and love.

People want blessings that bring freedom—not only from physical trouble and behavioral vice, but also from fear and lack. Freedom from danger, grief, depression, poverty, hunger, and abuse. Freedom from skill-set limitations, family and relationship discord, financial distress, closed doors, and road blocks. Freedom that lifts us up and gives us wings.

Yes, we could expand the meaning of *healing* to include all those types of blessings. And Christian Science practitioners do extend help to people on this basis every day. But the word *healing* evokes a more narrow meaning to people outside the Church: healing of physical troubles. Non-Christian Scientists hear the word *healing* from Christian Scientists and naturally associate the word with the people who "don't go to doctors" and choose an alternative to medical practice for health care. Which is in line with the everyday meaning of *healing* implied by Eddy's call for her Church to "reinstate primitive Christianity and its lost element of healing." And though this lost element of healing also includes releasing people from sin and reforming their character, still, the word *healing* somehow falls short of embracing a larger concept of the types of good in our lives that we all desire.

The word *healing* conveys that something wrong was either adjusted or needs adjustment, so while healing is sometimes needed, characterizing Christian Science primarily in terms of healing strikes me as a bit like characterizing mathematics in terms of *correcting*. Correcting math errors serves to support the practice of mathematics but isn't mathematics itself. In fact, correcting resides outside of the science of mathematics.

So it makes sense to me that Eddy chose the words *health* and *blessings* as the go-to words in her textbook's title and opening line.

At the theological heart of Christian Science lies the concept that we are already perfect, because we're 100% spiritual. Her discovery shows that little more than an "optical illusion of consciousness" (to borrow Einstein's phrase) reports otherwise and says we're broken, ill, unsound, and out of whack. So, hard as it may be to grasp, in our real and present state of being: No healing required. Anymore than "healing" would be required to fix what you see when you look at yourself in a circus funhouse mirror and see yourself outrageously distorted. You easily reject that image as bogus. You simply stick to what you know is true. You don't have to do anything physical. Just mental. You square what you think, how you see yourself, with what's true. The same basic principle underlies the metaphysical system of Christian Science: You square what you think and how you see yourself with Truth.

Which angle is more in line with that core concept of our current spiritual perfection? Emphasizing that Christian Science is about healing? Or emphasizing that Christian Science is about health and other blessings—freedom: about leaning on "the sustaining infinite," Principle, which upholds us and enables us to soar?

WHY, HOW, WHAT

Imagine Christian Scientists unified along these lines:

Why: In everything we do—we believe in challenging the status quo of materiality. In everything we do, we believe in leaning on the sustaining infinite: Spirit. We believe in helping people learn the truth about Life and how to walk in accord with what they learn. We believe in helping people live Scientifically—in sync with the laws of Mind, Life. In everything we do, we believe in helping people experience what naturally follows from living this way: health and other blessings—freedom. We believe in challenging the downward pull of mortality and helping people soar.

How: Through practitioners, teachers, books, periodicals, websites, lectures, and church services that bring people the proven metaphysical system of Christian Science, which teaches people how to effectively pray.

What: By relying on divine power, we heal people of illness and sin and rescue people from all types of trouble. We help others do what we ourselves seek to do—and what Mary Baker Eddy urged (*Science and Health*, p. 419): "Meet every adverse circumstance as its master."

Recall Simon Sinek's heads up: Successful organizations don't focus on "what." They focus on "why."

Imagine if a Christian Scientist at an Annual Meeting of The Mother Church said, "We know that everything in Christian Science is about helping people lean on 'the sustaining infinite.' About helping people lean on Spirit and experiencing what happens when you do: health and other blessings—freedom. As Mary Baker Eddy wrote (*Science and Health*, p. 258), 'God expresses in man the infinite idea forever developing itself, broadening and rising higher and higher from a boundless basis.' We know that everything in Christian Science is about helping people develop and broaden and rise higher and higher without limits—and experiencing health and other blessings as they do."

Yes, Eddy rooted Christian Science in Jesus's call to his disciples and everyone who wants to follow him today: "Heal the sick . . . raise the dead, cast out devils" (Matthew 10:8). Christian Science shows how to do that. It brings to humanity the power of Truth to heal human minds and bodies. And healing will remain a core mission of Christian Science for as long as humanity needs help. But healing is the "what" of Christian Science, not its "why."

And people don't buy what you do—they buy why you do it.

I don't practice Christian Science primarily because I seek physical healing or seek to heal others physically. I practice Christian Science primarily because this metaphysical system shows me the age-old benefits that come from putting my trust in Mind. Christian Science presents the deep truth about Life, revealing that Life is God—our eternal divine Principle, which possesses all power. Christian Science teaches me how to live in alignment with and benefit from this underlying, regulating, and governing Truth, which sustains my health and brings other tremendous blessings, including clarity, originality, foresight, insight, and joy, as well as the potential to "Meet every adverse circumstance as its master" in every area of my life and break through to freedom.

And consider the Blueprint of Eternal Reality (as I like to call it) that Eddy discovered: True Life—the substance of which is Spirit not matter—doesn't include adversity. True Life is led by well people, not by people in need of healing. In the House of Eternal Reality, perfect spiritual beings enjoy lives of continuous harmony governed by the divine Science of Life—just as numbers enjoy continuous harmony governed by the human science of mathematics. And here's the kicker: These perfect spiritual beings are you and I. Right now. Yes, *right now*—despite the way things seem (despite an "optical illusion of consciousness")—we are spiritual beings enjoying non-stop happiness, love, and well-being, abounding in limitless creativity, humor, perspicacity, goodwill, and zest. Right now, we are experiencing Life, trouble-free and healthy. Eternal Mind radiates us as naturally, continuously, completely, and coeternally—healthily and individually—as the sun radiates its sunbeams. According to the Storyboard of Eternal Reality: We don't need healing.

The core "why" of Christian Science? To put us in touch with this present Eternal Reality.

So ask yourself: *Why* do you exist? *Why* do you live?

To what degree does your true, eternal purpose and fulfillment in Life involve healing?

Versus: To what degree does your true, eternal purpose and fulfillment in Life involve soaring?

Purpose and fulfillment begin with "why."

Why do we live?

We live to soar.

And through the infinite galaxies of time, space, and place, we can trust that the Science of Life, which Christian Science reveals, will forever maintain us and sustain us, ensure our health and other blessings, and operate eternally to keep us aloft. Safe. On course.

Free as the birds.

> The term Science, properly understood, refers only to the laws of God and to His government of the universe, inclusive of man. From this it follows that business men and cultured scholars have found that Christian Science enhances their endurance and mental powers, enlarges their perception of character, gives them acuteness and comprehensiveness and an ability to exceed their ordinary capacity. The human mind, imbued with this spiritual understanding, becomes more elastic, is capable of greater endurance, escapes somewhat from itself, and requires less repose. A knowledge of the Science of being develops the latent abilities and possibilities of man. It extends the atmosphere of thought, giving mortals access to broader and higher realms. It raises the thinker into his native air of insight and perspicacity.
>
> —Mary Baker Eddy, *Science and Health*

Picture billboards that say:

THE CHURCH OF CHRIST, SCIENTIST—
Helping people lean on "the sustaining infinite"
—since 1879.

CHRISTIAN SCIENCE—
Bringing people health and other blessings—
freedom—since 1866.

O

Helping people . . .

S

r

a

If you want to build a ship, don't drum up the people to gather wood, divide the work, and give orders. Instead, teach them to yearn for the vast and endless sea.
—Antoine De Saint-Exupery, *The Little Prince*

Science operates eternally to keep us aloft. On course. Safe. Free.

7

Free The Angel

Get in sync with the source of your *unlimited* creative power.
Metaphysically-based insights that GPS me along the twists and turns of my life-road in art.

METAPHYSICAL WARRIOR

PUBLIC

TO ME, WRITING FEELS LIKE PAINTING. You prime the canvas with a few bold word-moves here and there then paint with freedom and verve and let it rip with stream of consciousness paint then paint over what you don't like and paint some more in bold ways to discover what you do like, and you stay with it, balancing improvisation and craft on the bedrock of judgment as you see the canvas turn from blank to "looks promising" to "that isn't so good" to "maybe if I stay with that part there and run with that and keep going . . ." Then—finally: "Ah, hey, I kind of like it now. Yes! That's what I had in mind!"

And all I did was free the angel.

I wrote the following essay, which I titled, "Free the angel," just before leaving my nine-year post as a senior writer and editor and the creative director for sister magazines of *The Christian Science Monitor*. I added this tagline after the title: "Get in sync with the source of your *unlimited* creative power." The essay appeared in the *Christian Science Sentinel*.

Every project I work on begins with those three words—*Free the angel*. Whether I'm creating a painting, a building, or an essay (like this one), those three words remind me to follow in the spirit of Michelangelo, who summed up his artistic method this way: "I saw the angel in the marble and carved until I set him free."

This great Italian sculptor, painter, and architect started with the end in mind. He knew that the angel already existed. He carved away everything that didn't bring out the ideal image he held in thought so he could simply reveal that ideal. He could set the angel free because the angel was already there.

Michelangelo's description of the angel in stone leads us to a grander metaphysical insight. Mary Baker Eddy defined angels in *Science and Health with Key to the Scriptures* (p. 581), as "God's thoughts passing to man; spiritual intuitions . . . the inspiration of goodness . . ."

Well, those angels surround us. They're already here. At every moment, Soul-radiating spiritual intuitions and good inspirations cut through the fog of mortality and stir us to dance and drum and film and act and paint, architect, cook, write, compose, and sing with beauty and awe and fire and grace.

Creative expression already exists within us, flowing freely and continuously from Soul—God—the source of unlimited, even breathtaking, artistic talent, skill-set mastery, and creative power.

All we have to do is carve away everything that doesn't look like the ideal of who we really are. Sculpt until we set ourselves free. Sculpt until we feel the deep presence and power of Soul, which releases us from anything that inhibits our freedom. Sculpt until we set ourselves free.

I've found that when I do that—when I "free the angel" within myself through scientific prayer—it's a whole lot easier to release the angel in my work.

This approach can work for everyone, and not only for artists, but also for those who design everything from industrial robots to tractors to computers, as well as for those who design other aspects of life, from a lesson plan to a PhD dissertation, from a conference to a business start-up, from a menu to a brand-new culinary creation. No matter what aspect of creativity you're called to bring to whatever you do, you can remember: Free the angel.

CHISEL THOUGHT

If to "free the angel" within ourselves requires us to sculpt our consciousness and reveal our ideal nature, the question comes down to this: What do you think your ideal nature is? Who do you think you are, relative to the actual source of creative power?

Are you personally the source? Or is the source greater than you? From where does our creativity and originality, our artist signature and voice, our evolving mastery and development—as well as our appreciation of art—spring? From a material brain? From a combination of a material brain and a personal, uniquely endowed soul? Or do our creative resources and energies spring from a bottomless reservoir, from one universal divine Soul that knows no foreshortened horizons, only horizons of infinity; no road blocks, only open highways of freedom;

no plateaus of talent and skill, only mountaintops of mastery? Soul that shines brighter than all the stars in all the galaxies of an infinite universe. Soul *unlimited*.

Turning to sources other than Soul can dead-end in frustration and despair, rivalry, envy, and ego trips pinballing between inferiority and superiority complexes. But choose Soul—choose to see yourself accurately as the expression of divine Spirit, for which Soul is a synonym—and Soul will shape thought and remove all that's unlike the angel in you.

Watch egotism, anxiety, and ambition fall away. You'll feel fueled by the "Soular" energy of courage, confidence, and calm exhilaration as you gaze into a light-filled universe of endless possibilities. Soul-generated creativity will flow to you and through you as surely as a magnet sticks to steel. See yourself (and others) as the unique and endlessly talented expression of the one Soul, and you'll feel the assurance of the Bible's God-sourced message of boundless potential and fulfillment (Rev 3:8): "I know thy works: behold, I have set before thee an open door, and no man can shut it."

We might also ask ourselves this: How does our one universal Soul, God, see us? Does Soul see us as vulnerable, physical beings, subject to trouble, decline, and death? Unlike Soul?! Or does Soul see us as entirely spiritual and therefore indestructible, immortal, and empowered? Logically, like produces like. Gaining this perspective enables us to see our ideal nature even more clearly.

Everyone has a choice to make about how to see themselves—as material or spiritual—and where to turn for inspiration and artistic light: either to the shipwreck shoals of materiality or the uplifting Soul-waters of spirituality. Will personal ego or universal Soul chisel thought?

BLAZE A NEW TRAIL

You can take the well-marked path or blaze a new trail. Robert Frost's 1920 poem "The Road Not Taken" gets at this choice. Frost encourages us to see how taking the road less traveled can make all the difference. In my work as an architect and painter, I've chosen to take a road less traveled. And I chalk that up to my trust that Soul, Mind, Life (synonyms for God), which inspires the explorer-desire in me, will also surely fulfill this desire.

And sure enough, hoping for and expecting to follow the road less traveled has made all the difference in my growth and development artistically and in the surprising richness of my experience.

And as we each travel our unique road, again the Bible assures us that we'll be OK: "Behold, I send an Angel before thee, to keep thee in the way, and to bring thee into the place which I have prepared" (Ex 23:20). I figure that's true not only for Moses, but for everyone—always. Soul's "spiritual intuitions" go before us. Soul will bring us into the artistic place that Soul has prepared for us—so we can free the angel of our own unique art.

So delight in your unbreakable, scientific unity with Soul. Let Soul move you. Let Soul inspire you and compose, design, shape, form, and storyboard your life and artistic development. Let Soul paint the canvas of your life. [Don't run away from your genius. It flows from Soul!] Let Soul power you forward as you blaze a new trail.

EXPECT INCOME

A lot of artists struggle financially. But we can reject the "struggling artist" role because Soul doesn't intend misery for anyone. It's right for artists to earn enough money and other forms of supply to live modestly, if not to thrive! And what's worked for me is taking a clear mental stand that sees myself as far above mortality's fake rules. When we get a true, spiritual perception of reality, our daily life syncs with that reality in amazing ways. So when we get a strong grip on these two core aspects of spiritual reality—equilibrium and abundance—we can expect to see tangible proof of that combination in our lives.

The source of creativity and income is the same: Soul. Soul not only abundantly provides our creativity, but also abundantly provides opportunities for its expression and reward. Expect to see this spiritual law of supply and demand light up your life. Expect the demand for your talents to go hand in hand with the supply of your talents.

Expect income.

BE A METAPHYSICAL WARRIOR

This expectant outlook is a metaphysical outlook—an outlook attuned to life-principles invisible to the material senses but discernible by our spiritual sense. Without this metaphysical outlook, I'd probably be too hobbled and bummed to keep going. But instead: I've adopted these seven words by Mary Baker Eddy as my anthem (*Science and Health*, p. 419): "Meet every adverse circumstance as its master."

I remind myself daily of that demand, because more often than not, I tend to initially meet every adverse circumstance as a pawn [on the chess board of day-to-day living]. I get knocked back on my heels, flummoxed and discouraged about what's going on. But then I hit the switch. And I remember that we're God-empowered to meet adversity as its master!

Every artist—and everyone who aspires to grow and develop in the art of living—can prayerfully face adversity with the confidence of a metaphysical warrior. With spiritual strength and serenity, we can expect proof of divine Soul's total governing and coordinating power.

You can trust Soul to remove any roadblock, iron out any wrinkle, and coherently, creatively direct all elements in the design of our lives. Mount righteous rebellion against the unrighteous authority of adverse circumstances. Be a metaphysical warrior.

LISTEN

That's what I've learned: Listen. Then act. Listen to that quiet inner voice, because that's the voice of Soul prompting you to move ahead this way or that way. Or to hold off, and do nothing—yet. I've learned to trust that inner power, our hardwired Soul-based intuition. That trust keeps me relaxed and ready, always receptive to the shooting stars of insight and foresight, helps me sidestep land mines and go around barriers, guides me and protects me, and prompts me what to do and how to do it and if to do it and when to do it.

Listen.

Listening and following divine inspiration unchains thought from limitation and mediocrity. Instead, we feel propelled upward by Spirit-inspired aspirations for radical breakthroughs and excellence. Mind turns us away from the false concept of a brain-centered material being with a personal soul who's either gifted or not, well-connected or not, fortunate or not, to our true unlimited Soul-fueled—God-sourced and God-sustained—artistic power, originality, mastery, and freedom.

You can carve the block of marble of your life hoping to sculpt your identity into existence, or you can turn to Soul to release the angel of your creative voice that already exists, divinely initiated and complete.

So chisel thought, blaze a new trail, expect income, be a metaphysical warrior, listen first—and free the angel!

"Every day we slaughter our finest impulses. That is why we get a heartache when we read those lines written by the hand of a master and recognize them as our own, as the tender shoots which we stifled because we lacked the faith to believe in our own powers, our own criterion of truth and beauty. Every man, when he gets quiet, when he becomes desperately honest with himself, is capable of uttering profound truths. We all derive from the same source. There is no mystery about the origin of things. We are all part of creation, all kings, all poets, all musicians; we have only to open up, only to discover what is already there."
— HENRY MILLER | *Sexus*

WE ARE ALL SCULPTORS, WORKING AT VARIOUS FORMS, MOULDING AND CHISELING THOUGHT.

—MARY BAKER EDDY
Science and Health

"The world is but a canvas to the imagination." —Henry David Thoreau

"We have to do the best we are capable of. That is our sacred human responsibility. Anything less is unforgivable." —Albert Einstein
in Peter Moffat's screenplay for *Einstein and Eddington*

INNERMISSION
Infuse everything with poetry.

Departure Transformation Return

LIFE IS A SCIENCE PROJECT. We work in the laboratory of thought, and you can choose right this moment to assert the truth and expect proof.

Turn inward to Soul, and discover the angel of your creative voice that already exists. Turn inward to the fireball of Life, and tap the dazzling creativity and thunder-and-lightning purpose that belongs uniquely to you and blazes continuously at your core.

You can summon divine power as surely as a star beam can summon star power.

DEEP / **LEVEL UP**

The secret of abundance: Give.

"Advance the canvas all at once." —Paul Cézanne

"You could be a work of art / If you just go all the way."
—songwriter Sam Concepcion, Kung Fu Fighting

"Two roads diverged in a wood, and I, I took the one less traveled by. And that has made all the difference."
—Robert Frost, "The Road Not Taken"

Unlimited openness to experimentation = rocket fuel.

There's only one story: the primordial World-Story, told and retold . . . what Joseph Campbell discovered: "one shape-shifting story of the vision quest that transforms the world." (see p. 63)

—Richard Boleslavsky, *Acting: The First Six Lessons*

"ART IS PRAYER."
—Russell Simmons
author of *Super Rich*

SOAR WITHOUT LIMITS

START WHERE YOU ARE.
USE WHAT YOU HAVE.
DO WHAT YOU CAN.
—Arthur Ashe

WORK IS PRAYER.

"The only rules in art are the rules that we discover for ourselves."

Why?

A SUDDEN FLASH OF TRUTH. Why do I create? Why do I write, paint, design, architect, and make books?

Well, first, I do these things simply because these pursuits make me happy! I love work—*living in the now*—blissfully unaware of the outside world as I do my best to make something special and significant.

Second, I do these things to make a gift to humanity through research and art, hoping to strike a match that will add a flicker of light and delight to the world.

And third, I do these things, I suppose ultimately, to move people—uplift people! Ideally, to inspire people to produce works that will in turn inspire others along an endless shoreline of brilliance, imagination, and breakthroughs.

And thanks to Robert McKee's book, *Story*, I now have an even fuller concept of what I truly aspire to generate in an audience though my work: ***aesthetic emotion***.

Aesthetic emotion, McKee explains, is produced when art, unlike life, creates in us a sudden flash of truth. This sudden flash of truth stirs in us an awareness of the convergence of ideas and emotion. We experience the simultaneous presence of meaning and feeling.

Rely on **META-CARE**.

Face **E**very **A**dversity **R**ighteously as a **M**etaphysical **W**arrior

On another occasion [Mary Baker Eddy] spoke of the great possibilities which lay before us in our work as Christian Scientists. She said we should be instruments of much good to the world. One student replied, "Yes, if we have love enough." She responded, "Love alone is not sufficient. You must also manifest divine wisdom if you would be of real service to others."

—Rev. Irving C. Tomlinson, *Twelve Years with Mary Baker Eddy: Recollections and Experiences*

8
Wake-Up Call

Escape from the mortal matrix.

In the fall of 2000, Gail Gilliland, then managing editor of *The Christian Science Journal*, asked me to write a piece about art and Jesus's resurrection. That was two years before I went to Boston to start a nine-year stint as senior editor and writer for the *Journal*. At the time of Gail's invite, I'd already written dozens of articles on spirituality for the *Journal* and its sister periodicals *Christian Science Sentinel* and *The Christian Science Monitor*. As I recall, Gail was looking ahead to a spring 2001 issue on Easter and thought that my writing about art from the point of view of a Christian Scientist who is also an artist might yield fresh insights.

At the time, I was living in New York City, where I pounded out a short essay titled, "Advancing to a higher idea—from cross to crown," which I e-mailed to Gail. Unfortunately, the piece didn't get published. I suspect that the blunt depiction of a wounded Jesus in the celebrated Renaissance painting that I focused on struck Gail's editorial colleagues as too much for their readership to handle. But that's just my hunch.

I recently dug up my essay thanks to an offhand remark that I heard painter Richard Diebenkorn make in a short film about his work at the De Young Museum in San Francisco. I got hit by one of those *BAM!* moments when I heard Diebenkorn refer to "Piero." I extrapolated from Diebenkorn's passing mention of Piero to a larger conclusion: *Of course Diebenkorn was inspired by the Italian Renaissance master Piero della Francesca. Both painters celebrate the control and soul of an architect and an architect's deep regard for geometry. How could I not have seen until now how the influence of Piero filters through Diebenkorn's paintings!*

And so when I got home, I opened up my old essay on Piero that I hadn't read in almost 13 years. I still like the gist of what I wrote back then. And I decided to tuck the essay into this book.

So here it is. Slightly updated and retitled, "**Wake-Up Call**."

The Resurrection of Christ, Piero della Francesca. Fresco. 1463-65. 88.6 in. x 78.7 in.

As a painter and an architect, I'm on a quest to find what Mary Baker Eddy described in *Science and Health* (p. 264) as "glorious forms which we sometimes behold in the camera of divine Mind, when the mental picture is spiritual and eternal."

And I've found that as I turn to Mind on my quest to find those "glorious forms," I'm abundantly rewarded. I experience a steady flow of intelligence, inspiration, and insight. And sometimes I even get glimpses of "glorious forms"—though more often than not to this point in my career, glorious forms created by other artists!

Case in point: Piero della Francesca. I learned about this Italian Renaissance artist during my undergraduate years as an architecture major at Princeton, and today I count Piero among the painters most relevant to my work. The lucid architecture of his paintings flows from his regard for geometry as a primary device for organizing artistic elements. His mathematically inclined compositions and exquisite three-dimensional rendering of form have no doubt inspired countless artists over the past 550 years. Piero's influence filters through the masterworks of many 19th- and 20th-century avant-garde painters from French Post-Impressionist Georges Seurat to American Semi-Abstractionist Richard Diebenkorn. Perhaps most important of all was the influence of Piero on Paul Cézanne, Pablo Picasso, and Georges Braque. What these three artists saw in the cubic masses of Piero's cityscapes ultimately ignited a revolution in painting that we call Cubism.

Piero's work exerts an ongoing influence in my own art, not only by way of Cubism but also by way of the insights by architectural historian Thomas Schumacher's essay "Deep Space/Shallow Space" (*Architectural Review*, January 1987, pp. 37-42)—a must-read for visual artists. Schumacher zeroes in on Piero's small painting *The Flagellation of Christ* and unpacks the artistic device of the split screen, bridging the 500-year gap between Piero's paintings and the artistic production of 20th-century architect-painter Le Corbusier, who incorporates the split screen technique into his work and the photography of his work.

But while I and other architects and artists mine Piero's paintings primarily for what they teach about structure and form, his paintings endure as celebrated works of art because they also speak to viewers—artists and non-artists alike—through the beauty and force of the paintings' representational depictions and metaphorical meaning. When we look at a painting by Piero, we feel its uplifting symbolic power. We sense the artistic unity of his high-minded design and his depiction of iconic religious content. Through his pre-cinema cinematic sensibility, Piero created works of art that move us through their riveting fusion of form and story.

Which brings me to Piero's large fresco *The Resurrection of Christ*. One of the world's most admired portrayals of Jesus's resurrection, Piero's large fresco on the wall of the town hall in Sansepolcro (the fresco measures over six feet wide and seven feet high) presents an almost life-size freeze-frame of one of the events central to the theology of Christianity. I'm struck by the connection between Piero della Francesca's fresco and a line by Mary Baker Eddy on page 426 in *Science Health*. Alongside the marginal heading "Christian standard," her line reads, "The relinquishment of all faith in death and also of the fear of its sting would raise the standard of health and morals far beyond its present elevation, and would enable us to hold the banner of Christianity aloft with unflinching faith in God, in Life eternal."

Add to the mix how art historian Marilyn Lavin describes Jesus in Piero's fresco (*Piero della Francesca*, p. 37): "He stands erect inside his sarcophagus, with one foot poised on the ledge, holding the labarum, a standard of victory—in this case, over death—in his right hand."

Factor in this footnote: Though at odds with the Bible's description, painters often employed a Roman sarcophagus as Jesus's tomb.

And now we see more clearly what Piero depicts in his stark but graceful picture of Easter morning. Jesus has risen from his stone coffin in a beautiful salmon-hued shroud holding a red Greek cross on a white background—the Christian standard of victory over death.

The banner of Christianity alludes to the cross on which Jesus was crucified, but the fresco also shows Jesus wearing a golden halo-like crown. The pairing of cross and crown helps me more fully appreciate Eddy's choice of these two emblems as the trademark of Christian Science.

As to the cross, she wrote (*Science Health*, p. 238), "The cross is the central emblem of history. It is the lodestar in the demonstration of Christian healing,—the demonstration by which sin and sickness are destroyed."

And as to the crown, she wrote in *The First Church of Christ, Scientist, and Miscellany* (p. 162) that Jesus "taught mankind to win through meekness to might, goodness to grandeur,—from cross to crown, from sense to Soul, from gleam to glory, from matter to Spirit."

Eddy concluded that Jesus not only travelled through the cross of defeat to the crown of victory for his own sake, he also role-modeled the journey as a service to others: Jesus's cross-to-crown triumph shows you and me that we have the potential to experience the same triumph.

The cross and crown signify the double-nature of everyone's pathway through human experience. And we all have an inalienable spiritual right to experience cross-to-crown progress.

The more we turn to Spirit to break the spell of materialism, the more our cross experiences—trouble and darkness—give way to crown experiences—harmony and light.

The more we turn to Mind for divine wisdom to guide us, the more our trek through the human labyrinth will include victories over adversities, thereby forging our lives in the service of others, because our example will bolster other people's confidence that they can do the same.

As I study Piero's fresco, I see how he subtly threads the double-theme of cross and crown through the matrix of his painting. Look, for example, at the landscape behind Jesus. Could we associate the cross with the barren winter trees of the left side of the painting? And associate the crown with the lush spring trees on the right side?

Now look at the four Roman soldiers in the foreground—at the bottom of the painting. In varying states of oblivion, the soldiers "stand guard" at Jesus's tomb. As Lavin puts it, "Paradoxically, these guardians are blind to Christ, who himself seems all-seeing" (p. 108). Figuratively speaking, it is these soldiers, not Jesus, whom Piero has entombed. Dead to the world of Spirit, their comatose bodies display poses of instability, in marked contrast to the vital, rock-solid, upright figure of Jesus. Above his useless guards who look trapped in an earthbound trance, Jesus rises radiant and strong—alive. *Free!* Through poetry in paint, Piero presents us face to face with an undefeated metaphysical warrior.

If the lower third of the painting symbolizes a burial ground (cross), the upper third, which includes the banner and Jesus's head—with his halo appearing cloud-like in relation to the background sky—signifies heaven (crown). Piero ties Jesus's body to the terrestrial landscape of the painting's middle ground, emphasizing the importance of Jesus's humanity and earthly experience on his cross-to-crown ascent.

But by far the most obvious reference to the cross in Piero's painting involves Jesus's wounds. Four of these wounds resulted from the crucifixion. The fifth, on Jesus's right side, was caused by a lance, which is held by the second soldier from the right. The thrust from the lance was to verify that Jesus was dead.

Piero deftly subordinates the tilted lance to the upright banner of peace. He makes the lance look insubstantial by fading it into the landscape in the distance. Through these devices, Piero renders the lance important, but impotent. Jesus's resurrection proved that physical wounds don't have the power to violate the law of Life—the divine Principle, that Eddy defined as God. I see the five wounds as symbols of the five physical senses, because Jesus's resurrection marked a triumph over the false belief that life is physical. Scientifically speaking, the five physical senses can't perceive, create, or destroy Life, because Life—our Life—is no more physical than the principles of mathematics and geometry.

In *The Resurrection of Christ*, Piero makes time stand still. Acting in multiple roles as painter, geometer, and philosopher, this Renaissance idealist not only stages an historical event, he also infuses the event with layers of meaning that transcend time. The look and feel of the painting strikes us as archetypal and modern. It radiates qualities that are at once matter-of-fact and transcendent. By deftly conflating the three traditional genres of painting—portrait, still life, landscape—within a larger symbolic framework, Piero evokes in us a profound sense of calm. And at the same time, the painting pulses with energy. We feel the undeniable crosscurrents of sadness and hope. Disarray and harmony. Death and Life. As Jesus holds the soft, unfurled "banner of Christianity aloft with unflinching faith in God, in Life eternal," we sense that this Easter morning is a metaphor for the dawning in everyone's consciousness of a higher concept of Life: Life that rises above materiality's sleep-induced dream.

Jesus said (John 14:12), "The works that I do shall you do also."

So when I look at Piero's painting, I'm struck by its startling subtext: *Escape from the drowsy illusion, the death trap, of the mortal matrix. Wake up to your spirituality. Wake up to Life.*

"Truth is not a reward for good behavior,
nor a prize for passing some tests.
It cannot be brought about. It is the primary, the unborn,
the ancient source of all that is.
You are eligible because you are. You need not merit truth.
It is your own. . . . Stand still, be quiet."
— Indian spiritual teacher and philosopher Sri Nisargadatta Maharaj

**9
Dr. Truth**

What do Christian Scientists really do when they get sick?

METAPHYSICAL WARRIOR

My name is Jeffrey. I'm a Christian Scientist. And I go to a doctor.
I picture myself standing at a Wednesday evening Christian Science testimony meeting and kicking off my remarks with that AA-like confession. Most people know little about the religion launched in 1866 by Mary Baker Eddy, but they usually know that "Christian Scientists don't go to doctors."

True enough. Rather than rely on medical practitioners, as a rule, Christian Scientists turn in prayer to Spirit for their well-being, including physical health.

But let me tell you what I and the woman to whom I was married at the time chose to do in the spring of 2013 when she faced alarming physical trouble.

Just back from many weeks of worldwide travel, my wife grew concerned about irregular bodily functions that she thought might be due to food she ate in the Philippines or Hong Kong. She Googled to find out about what the trouble might be, and what she read made her very afraid. According to the online information, someone with her symptoms should go immediately to a hospital.

I myself felt a sudden jolt of fear and confusion when she told me that. I empathized with how she was feeling—doing her best, as an experienced metaphysician, to remain calm and brave but swallowing hard in the face of her apparent crisis. And I wasn't sure what to suggest would be in her best interest: rush to a hospital or stay put and pray—in other words, address the challenge metaphysically.

But I knew that if we were to choose to go to a hospital, we would not likely make that decision out of fear and panic. And very quickly, in a matter of minutes, I did three things that helped us gain a solid mental grounding and brought the first wave of clarity and calm.

First, I made myself very still and listened internally, mentally, for the prompting of divine intelligence. I trusted in my go-to Bible quote Psalms 71:1: "In thee, O Lord [divine Mind], do I put my trust: let me never be put to confusion." Instantly, confusion lifted. I felt a sense of peace, a calm confidence that we could stay open to the guidance of Mind—Wisdom, divine Love—which would impel us to act in sound ways. And if Wisdom/Love were to prompt us to go to a hospital—as reluctant as we would typically be to go—OK. But if Wisdom/Love were to prompt us instead to pray as we had so many times successfully throughout our lives: also, OK. And it seemed to me clear in that moment that we ought to practice what we knew from our study and practice of Christian Science unless and until my wife decided that she wanted to go to a hospital.

Second, I wised up and saw that this adversity was yet another call for us to act as metaphysical warriors—to do what Mary Baker Eddy urged: "Meet every adverse circumstance as its master." And realizing that I'd already started to do that by turning to the Bible for inspiration, I shared this insight with my wife. We agreed that we were going to do what we were surely equipped to do: grasp what's true and expect proof.

Third, feeling encouraged to treat this adverse circumstance from my standpoint as a metaphysical master, I followed Eddy's instruction in how to treat a case through metaphysics (*Science and Health*, p. 411): "Always begin your treatment by allaying the fear of patients. Silently reassure them as to their exemption from disease and danger. Watch the result of this simple rule of Christian Science, and you will find that it alleviates the symptoms of every disease. If you succeed in wholly removing the fear, your patient is healed."

I silently reassured my wife—and verbally encouraged her to silently reassure herself—that she was indeed exempt from danger and disease, because she isn't material: She is forever the radiance of Spirit, a spiritual concept sustained and maintained by Mind, regulated and structured by Principle, safeguarded and protected by Love.

I silently reassured her that she coexists with Life—healthy and harmonious—as a sunbeam coexists with the sun. (Spirit, Mind, Principle, Love, and Life are some of the synonyms for God that Mary Baker Eddy explains in *Science and Health*.) My wife called a Christian Science practitioner and asked her to pray too. We then spent an hour of deep and enlightened prayer.

The turning point came when we read that week's Bible Lesson published in *The Christian Science Quarterly*. I read the lesson aloud while my wife rested in bed. This line from *Science and Health* (pp. 425-426), which neither of us recalled reading before, though surely we must have, lay in wait to aid us: "Discard all notions about lungs, tubercles, inherited consumption, or disease arising from any circumstance, and you will find that mortal mind, when instructed by Truth, yields to divine power, which steers the body into health."

We paused on the last part of that sentence, working through it for some time, marveling at what Eddy was telling us: ". . . you will find that *mortal mind, when instructed by Truth, yields to divine power, which steers the body into health.*"

I pictured a sea captain at the helm of a ship continuously steering his vessel into safe waters. I saw so clearly that the captain at the helm of my wife's health, as well as my own health, is divine Truth. Through our prayer, the human mind—afraid and confused—was being instructed by Truth and therefore yielding to divine power, which we could trust to steer my wife's body into health.

Now as to the cause and effect relationship between the human mind and the human body? Here's an analogy that has always helped me. When we watch a movie in a theater, the illusion of a substantial, three-dimensional world can seem so real that we feel we inhabit that world. But we know better. And we know that if we wanted to alter what we see on screen, we would have to go to the projection room and change the film. Because we can only see on screen what we run through the projector. Likewise, when we look at ourselves, the illusion of a substantial, three-dimensional body can seem so real that we feel we inhabit that body. But the human body has no more substance, self-action, and reality than does a movie projected on a screen. The human body is a mental projection of the human mind. When it comes to the relationship between the human mind and the human body, the human mind is a movie projector, and the human body is a movie. The concepts embedded in the human mind are the movie reel. If we want to see a better movie, we have to change the reel.

We have to swap out the movie reel of materiality for the movie reel of spirituality. Swap out the movie reel of false beliefs for the movie reel of truth.

When the human mind relinquishes a false sense of life as matter-based and physical, and yields to the harmonizing influence of Truth, the human mind becomes imbued with a higher concept of life as purely spiritual—beautiful, harmonious, and healthy in form and function. And we then see a better movie. The body will become more beautiful, harmonious, and healthy in form and function.

As we prayed and thought through these ideas during this episode of my wife's adversity, we understood how a change in her outlook, a more elevated, spiritual viewpoint—an improvement in the complexion of the human mind, which gradually becomes less opaque and more transparent to the light of Truth—could naturally lead to an improvement in the body.

I then said something that my wife credits for lifting the dark clouds of fear and false responsibility: "You don't have to do anything, darling. You are in the hands of the Great Physician, who is caring for you, treating you, tending to your every need. *You* don't have to do anything. Anymore than you would have to do anything if you were in a hospital. You would do nothing except trust the doctor to take care of you."

And I added, "Darling, you are right now under the expert care of a doctor you can trust: Dr. Truth."

At that point, my wife's fear evaporated. A feeling of total reassurance and serenity came over us. We were 100% clear about our choice of whether to head to a hospital: No. My wife was right where she needed to be—in the hospital of divine consciousness, under the constant supervision of Dr. Truth, head of surgery and all other care departments, including the emergency room. My wife could rest assured that all that needed to be done on her behalf was being done—because through the influence of Truth in human consciousness, divine power "steers the body into health."

Dr. Truth assured us that my wife, despite the misleading mortal picture, is spiritual and therefore whole and healthy—"exempt from danger and disease." She could no more experience trouble than a star beam, because like a star beam, my wife coexists with and expresses the harmony of her source: divine and eternal Life.

I told my wife that there was nothing more we needed to do. We could do as Einstein did on the eve of the solar eclipse when his theory of gravity was on the line: He was so certain that his grasp of science was correct that rather than wait up with other scientists to see if his theory was going to be proved correct, he confidently and serenely just went to bed.

In our situation, we had taken a principled stand against adversity—a principled stand grounded in divine Principle, in Truth. And on this basis—this scientific basis, the basis of sound metaphysics—we met adversity as its master. We had grasped the truth—and could now expect proof. So like Einstein, we confidently and serenely went to bed. My wife assured me that she felt secure in the care of Dr. Truth.

Remember: Eddy assures us that if we succeed in wholly removing the fear, then the patient is healed. So you can imagine how grateful we were—but not surprised—the next morning when my wife reported a change in her physical condition. She was completely healed.

That morning, as I sat on our front porch, I felt an influx of humility and awe as I considered how the influence of Truth had reversed the mortal picture from bad to good. When we first encountered this adversity, we didn't see that meeting it fearlessly and with confidence in metaphysical treatment would bless us and help us take a few more thought-steps forward through the Labyrinth of the human condition. We also didn't anticipate that what started out as a critical need for help for my wife resulted in giving us a handle on the big picture of our health care—health care that not only rescues us in times of distress but also monitors and maintains our ongoing well-being.

"For the first time," I e-mailed my wife at her office later that day, "I see and feel that we *do* go to a physician. A full-time Physician. We *are* under a Doctor's care. At all times. I realized last night that our spiritual support team is bigger than I thought: We've not only got a full-time Creative Director, Storyboard Artist, Counsellor, Mentor, Manager, Talent Agent, Financial Planner, Banker, and Pilot working overtime for us behind the scenes—we've also got a full-time Physician who tenderly and skillfully attends to our health care every moment. All we have to do is see that, get that, feel that, and absolutely rest, relax, and trust in that reality. Then surely, through the natural law of cause and effect, we will experience proof, because this insight into the science of life flows from the inspiration of Truth. And Truth is manifesting itself in our lives through its impact on our human minds and bodies."

After I sent that e-mail, I wrote a note to myself: "Imagine how safe many people would feel if they were under the 24-hour care of a physician. Well, Jeffrey, you *are*—right now, at all times. Your divine Physician provides continuous in-home service, as well as travel service—wherever you go, wherever you are, every moment of your days and nights. (And for free.) So there's nothing to fear—ever. All is well. And all *always* will be well throughout your life. You and your loved ones are under your Physician's constant care, beneficiaries of the tangible, ongoing flow of well-being.

"So, Jeffrey, change your point of view: You *do* go to a doctor. You go to the one divine Master Doctor: Truth. You've wisely placed yourself in Truth's care. And Truth's instruction right within your own consciousness is working all the time on your behalf, impelling you to discard faith in the earthly clay of medical predictions, diagnoses, and treatments and yield to the heavenly sunlight of divine power, inspiring you to uplift your consciousness from matter to Spirit—thereby naturally restoring your body, even creating and structuring a better body, and safeguarding and preserving your health. So feel the serenity, confidence, and comfort that flows from this realization. Rest and rejoice in this amazing provision. Your divine Physician's got you covered."

Some weeks later, on the road to San Francisco, I said to my wife, "Let's come up with a name for our spiritual health-care plan." We thought for a moment, and then it hit me: *Meta-care*.

And the dots connected.

A universal spiritual program under the auspices of Dr. Truth (who heads every department, from the emergency room to anaesthetics, from surgery and maternity to intensive care and therapy), Meta-care covers everyone. No exclusions for pre-existing conditions. No deductibles. No copays or delays. All we need to do? Sign up. In other words: Lean on Truth. As Jesus said (John 8:32), "And ye shall know the truth, and the truth shall make you free."

DEPARTURE, TRANSFORMATION, RETURN

Like so many challenges and opportunities that we encounter throughout our lives, the true story I just told about my wife and me unfolds along the lines of the Hero's Journey described by Joseph Campbell in *The Hero With A Thousand Faces* and transposed by Hollywood story consultant Christopher Vogler in *The Writer's Journey* (as I explain in Chapter 1). By way of illustration, let me break down our story into the 12 stages that Vogler identifies. These 12 stages—Campbell lists 17—span the archetypal three-act structure of the hero's adventure: Departure, Transformation, Return.

DEPARTURE: My wife and I start the adventure in our **Ordinary World**, our lives in balance, unafflicted by adversity. We then experience a sudden event—my wife's physical trouble—that throws our ordinary world out of balance, signaling a **Call to Adventure**. At first confused and frightened, and tempted to do something that cuts against the grain of who we really are—we freeze: We **Refuse the Call**. But then after turning to Mind for inspiration and clarity—after **Meeting with the Mentor** (the word *mentor* derives from the same root as the word *mind*)—we feel our spirits lift. Our doubts and fears begin to subside. We sense revitalized courage and purpose, and we find ourselves willing—eager—to answer the call to adventure and live true to the pledge of the metaphysical warrior: "Meet every adverse circumstance as its master" (Mary Baker Eddy, *Science and Health*, p. 419). "Game on," we shout. And we begin our brave quest—**Crossing the First Threshold** from our Ordinary World of limiting human perspectives, we step into a Special World that offers enlarged spiritual understanding.

TRANSFORMATION: Now fully committed to our journey and our goal, we move forward in prayer, encountering along our way **Tests, Allies, Enemies**. We find our courage and confidence periodically tested as we recall what Christian Science has taught us and as we search for what we need to know metaphysically to return home with the prize of healing. On guard against our mortal enemies of resurgent fear, resistance, doubt, and confusion, we gain strength and confidence, serenity, and assurance, from our allies: inward messages of Truth. These allies assure us that the labyrinth through which we find our path to healing is thoroughly known. We stay true to what Campbell calls "the hero way of thought" (*The Hero With A Thousand Faces*, p. 24)—and for us, *the hero way of thought is the metaphysical warrior's way of thought*. We press forward in our **Approach to the Inmost Cave**, where our deepest insights turn darkness to light and enable us to spiritually face down my wife's physical **Ordeal**. **Seizing the Sword** of Truth, we claim our **Reward**—healing.

RETURN: We retrace our footsteps back through and out of the labyrinth, recalling with awe what we have experienced. And we begin

The Road Back home. My wife's body has not yet conformed to our metaphysical breakthrough to healing, but we trust completely that this will happen—and soon it does. Balance restored. But we are not the same as when we set out. We have changed. Tested by the fire of experience, we are wiser and stronger. We possess new insights into Life, including a clearer view of who we really are and the true source of our power and well-being. We have travelled from the valley of darkness to the mountaintop of light, and while we do not experience a classic resurrection episode just before the finish line of our return, we do return having undergone a **Resurrection** of health and faith. We **Return with the Elixir** of transformation and enlightenment, hoping that through our telling of what we've learned, other people will benefit from our experience and feel more fully equipped with courage, acumen, and foresight to answer their Herald Call to Adventure and pursue their own brave quest.

PRIVATE

LIVE BRAVE.

> To discover the mode of life or of art whereby your spirit could express itself in unfettered freedom. . . . Yes! Yes! Yes! He would create proudly out of the freedom and power of his soul, as the great artificer whose name he bore, a living thing, new and soaring and beautiful, impalpable, imperishable.
> —James Joyce, *A Portrait of the Artist as a Young Man*

a Thought Paint

Personal brushstrokes on the canvas of life.

METAPHYSICAL WARRIOR

I'VE LEARNED TO STAY OPEN TO INSIGHTS AND FORESIGHTS that flow freely during good times and bad. I'm ready and eager for inspiration that shines through either blue skies or brewing thunderstorms.

And I tend to write down what hits me. So I'm constantly logging thoughts on my iPhone or iMac in web-based (iCloud) Apple Notes.

A mix of personal prayers and words of inspiration from others, these notes rev up my spirit and restore my soul, give meaning and force to my life, infusing it with clarity, fueling it with energy—making me feel like an engine firing on all cylinders.

I gain confidence, hope, and power as I make these notes. They help me feel on top of the situation, mentally, spiritually, emotionally. I feel equipped to face adversity, serenely aided by reminders of what Eddy called "the sustaining infinite."

Much of what I write down or send to others in e-mails is so insider—so individual and personal—that I hesitate to publish them, raising a series of questions: Where do you draw the line between private and public? What do you keep to yourself, and what do you share with others? How much of the truth as one sees it can one safely reveal?

In a way, this whole book raises these questions.

And I'm surer of the questions than I am of the answers.

But I'll take the risk and offer the following thought-fragments, a few of my architect-painter brushstrokes on life's philosophical canvas—thought-shield and thought-sword messages along my journey as a metaphysical explorer and metaphysical warrior.

Maybe these notes will also help you.

A note about JASON LEEZAC, to whom I refer frequently, oddly enough! He's a swimmer. And as a member of a US four-man relay team in the 2008 Summer Olympics, he suddenly, stunningly, within about 25 yards of the wall (the "finish line"), caught up with the world record–holder swimmer ahead of him as if lightning bolts of SPEED and UNWORLDLY POWER rocketed him through the water, snatching improbable victory, not only for himself but for the entire team, from what appeared to be the sure jaws of defeat. It was something to behold. Electrifying. Shocking, in fact. So that moment—code name "the Jason-Leezac moment" or "the Jason-Leezac principle"—lives with me as a symbol of that DIVINE LIGHTNING-BOLT POWER we can summon to aid us at all times, against all odds.

1. MIND REMOVES ALL ROADBLOCKS.

2. MIND CUTS THROUGH ALL DENSITY, RESISTANCE, AND RED TAPE.

3. MIND DISARMS ALL AGGRESSION, MISDIRECTION, HALF-TRUTHS, AND HIDDEN AGENDAS.

4. MIND DISSOLVES ALL CONFUSION AND RESOLVES ALL DILEMMAS.

5. MIND SUPPLIES HIGHER LEVELS OF COMPREHENSION and DEFUSES LOWER LEVELS OF COMPREHENSION THAT TRY TO BULLY AND FLUMMOX (confuse).

6. MIND ILLUMINATES. MOTIVATES, AND ANIMATES.

7. MIND SUPPLIES SERENITY—NOW.

I REJOICE IN THIS **TRUTH**! AND I CAN'T WAIT TO SEE TANGIBLE **PROOF**!

JEF7REY, TRUST THE **DIVINE CREATIVE DIRECTOR** to continuously design the storyboard of your life and give it special purpose and shape, coherent form and meaning, energy and serenity, dignity and delight, beauty and grace, precision, courage, and zing . . . through a perfect blend of CONTROL AND SOUL.

Your divine Creative Director unfolds—without confusion, hitch, roadblock, or delay—the *progressive* journey of your life, assuring that it will be influential, fruitful, prosperous, worthy, and ever-advancing toward new ideas, findings, and opportunities.
—*progressive* = moving forward or onward: advancing . . . making use of or interested in new ideas, findings, or opportunities

MOMENT BY MOMENT, RETURN TO YOUR ACTIVITIES IN THE POWER OF THE SPIRIT WITH THE CALM ASSURANCE THAT ALL IS WELL AND THAT YOU— AND EVERYONE—ARE CONTROLLED BY DIVINE INTELLIGENCE AND LOVE.

MY CONTINUOUS THEME: **FRUITION**.
I TRUST THE DIVINE FRUITION FORCE AT WORK IN MY LIFE—ANIMATING, ORCHESTRATING, AND AMALGAMATING MY ASPIRATIONS AND WORK.
(amalgamate = to unite or merge into a single entity)

I EXPRESS **TACT**: **T**OTAL **A**CUMEN **C**HARM AND **T**ACT.
I express complete and unified (Total) keenness and depth of perception (Acumen); compelling grace and attractiveness of manner (Charm); and sensitive mental and aesthetic perception (Tact "a"), as well as a keen sense of what to do or say to maintain good relations with others and avoid offense (Tact "b").

TRUST THE **DIVINE PUZZLE MASTER** to piece together the jigsaw of your life in amazing, productive, influential ways!

Line on a church message-board: "If God is your Copilot, swap seats!"

DIVINE LIFE/MIND: YOU THE PILOT. YOU THE WRITER, ARCHITECT, PAINTER, CREATIVE DIRECTOR, TALENT AGENT, BUSINESS MANAGER, OPPORTUNITY-PROVIDER, COMMUNICATOR.

TAKE NOTHING FOR YOUR JOURNEY TODAY—EXCEPT A SPIRITUALLY-MINDED, PURELY METAPHYSICAL VIEWPOINT. TAKE DISCERNMENT, CLARITY, FORESIGHT. GRACE, HUMILITY, SERENITY, INTEGRITY.
PUT ON THE WHOLE "MIREAFAAB-DTS"-PROOF ARMOR OF DIVINITY. (See p. 69.)

LOOKING AHEAD: MIND controls the events of this year and next. And nothing can block MIND's expression of well-being, clarity, and startling intelligence. Now let's anticipate and trust that we'll see honest to goodness proof. WAHOO IN ADVANCE!!!!!

RELY ON YOUR SPIRITUAL MIND'S DAZZLING POWER to SOLVE, DISSOLVE, AND RESOLVE—to SOLVE PROBLEMS, DISSOLVE CONFUSIONS, AND RESOLVE DILEMMAS . . . and PRODUCE ASTONISHING HARMONY AND CLARITY THAT SPIRALS INTO EVERY DETAIL OF YOUR LIFE.

FEAR NOT. YOU HAVE ALL GOOD NOW.
Here, Now, This Moment, MIND is creatively directing your mission, vision, and provision.

DIVINE LIGHTNING BOLTS of inspiration and guidance cut through the fog of human consciousness and strike every heart involved in your beautiful plan for me, O LIFE, MIND. And these lightning bolts strike my heart too, prompting me to do what others need to help further your beautiful plan for them. You prompt everyone to act together in just the right way—today and every day. You bring blessings to one and all. (Based on my article "Divine 'Lightning Bolts' Strike Every Heart" in the *Christian Science Sentinel*, June 23, 2003, pp. 14-15.)

NEVER ENTER THE RING WITHOUT STOPPING TO ADJUST YOUR SPIRITUAL ARMOR. KNOW THIS: **ONE MIND GUIDES AND GOVERNS US ALL**.

ENTER THE SPECIAL WORLD of SPIRITUALITY. Leave the ORDINARY WORLD of Materiality. In other words, BEWARE THE SEVEN DEADLY SINS: greed, sloth, anger, lust, pride, gluttony, envy. AFFIRM THE PRESENCE of THE SEVEN LIFE-GIVING VIRTUES: generosity, industry, poise, purity, humility, control, good will.

Remember, you are covered from the devourer by divine affection and protection—whether the devourer takes the form of the seven deadly sins or other types of trouble, including malice, injury, confusion, worry, and fear. I don't give these villains permission to infiltrate my consciousness or my day-to-day experience in any shape or form!

MIND/SOUL EXPRESSES EFFORTLESS MASTERY, naturalness, erudition, charm, poetry, quickness, spontaneity, imagination, and grace in everything that MIND/SOUL does. Therefore, I EXPRESS EFFORTLESS MASTERY, naturalness, erudition, charm, poetry, quickness, spontaneity, imagination, and grace in everything I do, and I demand to see this truth continuously expressed in my everyday life in practical ways. NOW.

"Be still, and know that I *am* God" (Psalms 46:10).

Be still and know: Here, Now, This Moment, I AM PERFECT, I AM GREAT, I AM A MASTER, "I AM GOD." I don't have to prove it. I don't have to earn it. It's a fact—a coefficient of Reality.

coefficient = a constant factor as distinguished from a variable (Thanks Kenny Werner for the assurance "I AM PERFECT, I AM GREAT, I AM A MASTER" from your amazing book *Effortless Mastery*.)

I AM GRATEFUL FOR STUNNING, TANGIBLE, AND RATIONAL PROOF OF **SOUL-POWER UNLIMITED!!!!!!!!!** THANK YOU, MIND/SOUL, FOR YOUR POWER AND INFLUENCE IN EVERY ASPECT OF MY LIFE.

GET IN HARMONY WITH LIFE'S SCIENTIFIC BASIS.
Get your consciousness (your viewpoint) in harmony or alignment with Life's scientific basis, and you will experience happiness, health, and freedom—and you will possess the power to help other people to do the same. But if you think or behave out of alignment with Life's scientific basis, then you can expect the same impact on your human experience as on a jet plane flying out of alignment with the science, or laws, of flight: trouble. What does it take to attain this alignment? A higher perspective. A spiritual, as opposed to a materialistic, perspective. A Scientific perspective that corrects the misperception of who you are.

I'M COUNTING ON MIND'S NIAGARA-LIKE POWER TO REMOVE EVERY ROADBLOCK ON THE ROAD AHEAD. I EXPECT EVERYONE INVOLVED TO FEEL MIND'S IRRESISTIBLE POWER, IMPELLING THEM TO DO WHAT NEEDS TO BE DONE—NOW!!!!! SO GET WITH THE PROGRAM: FEEL THE JASON-LEEZAC-TESTED *ELECTROVECTOR POWER OF MIND* WORKING IN YOU AND OTHERS TO GET GOOD STUFF DONE—AND TO GET IT DONE WITHOUT DELAY!!!!!!! MIND SENDS DIVINE LIGHTNING-BOLTS OF ILLUMINATION, MOTIVATION, AND ANIMATION THAT STRIKE THE HEART AND CONSCIOUSNESS OF EVERY PERSON CRUCIAL TO MY HERO'S JOURNEY. THESE *VIBROCIOUS LIGHTNING BOLTS OF CLARITY* CUT THROUGH ALL THE MUCK (APATHY, RESISTANCE, HOSTILITY, DENSITY, INERTIA, INEFFECTIVENESS, IMPOTENCE, and CONFUSION) TO BRING MARVELOUS AND SURE FULFILLMENT AND FRUITION!!!!!!!!!!! . . . AND **ABUNDANCE BEYOND MEASURE**. Here, Now, This Moment. THAT'S THE TRUTH. AND I EXPECT PROOF.

"In thee, O Lord [MIND], do I put my trust; let me never be put to confusion" (Psalms 71:1)—I know what to do, and I know how to do it. I know what to say, and I know how to say it. I know when to do it and if to do it. Because divine Mind knows, and divine Mind is my mind.

Which means: *I am not confused. I am not lost. I am not absentminded, feebleminded, or simpleminded.* This Mind—the *only* mind—continuously clarifies, crystallizes, calibrates, communicates, consolidates—thinks, designs, directs, guides, explores, and innovates. I coexist with this Mind, express this Mind, so *I demand to feel and experience the vivid presence of this Mind mentoring me moment by moment!*

Thanks to the book *The Law of Attraction* by Esther Hicks and Jerry Hicks, I now see more clearly that divine Principle's spiritually-based Law of Attraction is unfolding and orchestrating abundance in my life—and I am allowing it to happen. I am in the process of experiencing abundance here, now, this moment. I got it very clear during an hour-long stroll along the beach at twilight that I truly am at one with the Infinite, in harmony with the invisible structure and forces of Reality, that I am loved, and that I am truly destined to attract into my life significant Work, Creativity, Insight, Influence, and Abundance. I am allowing the lightning bolts of divine Mind to storyboard and orchestrate—to creatively direct—everything needed to experience these five things. ***I am in the process of experiencing significant Work, Creativity, Insight, Influence, and Abundance. Now!***

Hear the divine whisper: I COEXIST NOW AND FOREVER WITH IMMORTAL LIFE. I POSSESS (BY REFLECTION) ASTONISHING MIND-POWER AND SOUL-FIRE. I AM PERFECT, UNDER LOVE'S MANAGEMENT—BEAUTIFULLY DESIGNED AND 100% SUSTAINED, GUARDED, AND GUIDED BY DIVINE PRINCIPLE. I AM COVERED FROM THE DEVOURER OF RESISTANCE IN ANY FORM, BECAUSE I AM CLAD IN MONSTER-PROOF ARMOR. INVINCIBLE. THUNDERBOLTS OF FREEDOM, HEALTH, PROSPERITY, and FRUITION ELECTROVECTOR ME CONTINUOUSLY . . . **HERE, NOW, THIS MOMENT.**

LIKE THE NORTH-FORCE EXERTED ON THE NEEDLE OF A COMPASS, SPIRITUALITY—strength, grace, genius, happiness, health, and harmony—PULLS AT YOU. FEEL ITS PULL.

5 RANDOM NOTES:
1. Divine Principle sustains you, protects and directs you, actively and continuously storyboards your life with total Control and Soul.
2. Feel the deep presence and power of Life's reassuring radiance, manifesting through you aspiration and contentment, flexibility and resolve, promise and fulfillment—singing through you, in two-part harmony, intuition and reason, tranquility and verve, creativity and courage . . . imparting to you insight and foresight, empathy and strength, health and wealth—perspicacity, serenity, composure, resilience, and grace.
3. Infuse everything with spontaneity, excellence, poetry, and passion.
4. "The path of safety [**opportunity, wherewithal, fruition**] will open up for you from where you least imagine it." —Virgil, *The Aeneid*
5. "Hold on tight" to metaphysical truth, but "hold on loose" to the ways that you feel this truth ought to play out in your life.

deus ex machina: an ancient Greek story strategy for a sudden and random intervention by divine Power, often to tie up the loose ends of an otherwise irresolvable struggle and to rescue the hero from disorientation, ambiguity, disfavor, irresolution, trouble, and doom. Think of deus ex machina as thunderbolts of divine Principle cutting through the darkness of the mortal dream and lifting you to the Light, rescuing you—suddenly—from banality and danger, opening a new door to Happiness, Abundance, and Good, arranging a whole constellation of events and circumstances, for which all experiences to this point have been graciously preparing you.

Trust your **DIVINE CHESS MASTER** to make creative and clever moves (winning moves!) in the chess game of your life—to **MASTER MIND** brilliant moves that will dazzle you. And benefit others.

Architect me. Design my life-journey in accord with Your Purpose and Plan. Weave the threads of my life into a beautiful tapestry.

CONTROL AND SOUL—the basis of design, whether visual or verbal, whether art or life.

FEEEEEEL the divine energy of Spirit bringing you into NEWNESS, ABUNDANCE, HEALTH, FRUITION and HAPPINESS. The **Fish's Mouth Principle** of ABUNDANCE is ever-ACTIVE in your life right now. LOVE'S UNLIMITED POWER CONTINUOUSLY BALANCES THE SCALES OF TALENT and OPPORTUNITY, OPPORTUNITY and FULFILLMENT, FULFILLMENT and INCOME—AS WELL AS ACCOMPLISHMENT and RECOGNITION.

FLOW STATE SYNERGY—FSS (FS^2!): that in-the-pocket same-wavelength comfort-zone forward-momentum flow-state feeling you have with someone that makes you realize you're not alone. Whatever you call it—PLS (Parallel Lines Synergy) or CSP (Copacetic Synergy Power) or PLCS (Parallel Lines Copacetic Synergy) . . . or IMPACT (Integrated Mutual Precision Alignment by Cosmic Tuning)—it's MAGIC! Bliss.

LIFE IS FAIR because LIFE IS GOD, our PRINCIPLE, TRUTH, and LOVE—and PRINCIPLE IS FAIR; TRUTH IS FAIR; LOVE IS FAIR. THEREFORE LIFE IS FAIR. It may *seem* otherwise. So challenge the impotent fraud of mortal belief that says life is unfair with the mighty sword of this spiritual counter-fact: **LIFE IS FAIR!**—HONEST, JUST, TRUST-WORTHY, FULL, KIND, GOOD, FREE. SO EXPECT TO FEEL, EXPRESS, and EXPERIENCE THIS TRUTH. NOW.

LIFE is an invisible eternal Principle that governs all of us in practical, good ways. Divine Principle is power. The *only* power. And this power paints our lives with beautiful fireworks of opportunity and victory.

YOU ARE MOTIVATED AND GUIDED BY MISSION, PRINCIPLES, GOALS, AND VISION—BY THE TWIN STARS OF PASSION and CONTRIBUTION. (Inspired by *First Things First* by Stephen R. Covey, A. Roger Merrill, Rebecca R. Merrill)

FEEEEL THE TRANSCENDENT LIGHTNING-BOLT POWER —THE TENDER "BAM!"—OF INFINITE MIND.

"A knowledge of the Science of being . . . raises the thinker into his native air of insight and perspicacity" (Mary Baker Eddy, *Science and Health*, p. 28). Perspicacity = acute mental vision. **Perspicacious implies unusual power to see through and understand what is puzzling.** We all have it: MIND-supplied perspicacity, MIND-clarifying insight and discernment, MIND-powered ACUTE MENTAL VISION to see through and understand what is puzzling—and do something about it.

Mind mentors and guides you continuously as you blaze a daily path toward creative, intuitive, and inspired decision-making. Stay true to your Soul/Mind-inspired motto: GIVE YOURSELF CHOICES. Always stay open to new ideas, surprising solutions, and serendipity. (And remember: If it doesn't make sense, get it to make sense—it's *always* consequential.)

LEAN ON MIND'S NIAGARA-LIKE POWER to shape your life. (Hear the ROAR!!!) The Creative Spirit expresses me, moves me, employs me, safeguards me, upholds me, fulfills me, preserves me, enlarges me, strengthens me, helps me, and designs every aspect of my journey along the unpredictable highway ahead.
You are in the process—HERE NOW THIS MOMENT—of feeling, experiencing, and celebrating . . . ta-da:
REMEDY and ABUNDANCE (*remedy* implies removing or making harmless a cause of trouble, harm, or evil).

THE DIVINE INFLUENCE IS ALL POWERFUL IN YOU. Feel the breath of almighty LIFE exhaling good into every facet of your being and lifting you up on wings of fruition, courage, wisdom, and peace.

In the end, you need little to put the ship of life on an even keel: spirituality and trust in Principle and Mind. Like an eternal flame, this spirituality and trust burn within you and can't be extinguished. But if you resist their power—and the limitless capacities that spring from spirituality and trust in Principle and Mind—then your adventure into life's labyrinths may prove hopeless and without light.

I looked up the word *meekness*: enduring injury with patience and without resentment. Then I looked up the word *patience*:
1. bearing pains or trials calmly or without complaint
2. manifesting forbearance under provocation or strain
3. not hasty or impetuous
4. steadfast despite opposition, difficulty, or adversity
5. able or willing to bear

Draw continuously from the deep well of meekness and patience. These qualities are innate to your true, spiritual nature. Give way to them. Let meekness and all five definitions of patience shape your motives and thoughts—your actions and reactions—in the face of adversity.

And at the same time, be wise and brave. Remember the Serenity Prayer: "God grant us the serenity to accept the things we cannot change, courage to change the things we can, and wisdom to know the difference."

Turn inward to MIND to GPS you in your work. MIND enables you to blend analysis and intuition, preparation and improvisation, imagination and craft, and MIND equips you to adapt, regroup, retreat, advance, anticipate, and persevere through the night to the finish line.

The Hero's Journey shows that adversity happens. *Especially when you try to move forward.* But behave like a Metaphysical Warrior: "Meet every adverse circumstance as its master" (Eddy). **F**ace **E**very **A**dversity **R**ighteously. Turn inward to Spirit for peace and strength. Feel Mind's correcting power and sustaining influence. Trust Love to serve and protect you . . . and carry you safely through the night.

Don't be afraid. Get a grip on **F.E.A.R.**
Love supplies you with courage, timing, and guile (cunning intelligence) to **F**ace **E**very **A**dversity **R**ighteously as a Metaphysical Warrior.
Righteousness = right thinking.
And right thinking equips a metaphysical warrior to do what Mary Baker Eddy urged: "**M**eet **E**very **A**dverse **C**ircumstance **A**s **I**ts **M**aster." *Not as its scared and bullied victim! As Its Master!*
Code word: **MEACAIM**.

Trust **YOUR SPIRITUAL MIND**, the only Mind there really is —the one Mind behind everything, *your* Mind—to systematically, creatively storyboard, design, direct, and develop your aspirations, purpose, talents, skills, opportunities, achievements, and impact.

I receive e-mails now and then from readers of the Christian Science magazines thanking me for one of my articles. I recently received two such e-mails within a 24-hour period. One from a painter in England who thanked me for an article that I wrote in 2011 for the *Christian Science Sentinel,* "Free the Angel." The other from an author in Germany who thanked me for an article I wrote in 2008 for *The Christian Science Journal.* She said, "Your article on 'Intelligence Now' continues to be a keeper in our family. . . . You should know about this. . . . Your influence reaches across the Atlantic right into downtown Berlin."

In my thank-you e-mail to the church friend in Germany, I said:
. . . and to think that only yesterday, when feeling a bit down about how little I've done in the face of all I hope to do and wish I could do, I was brought back to my senses when I marveled at Love's assurance through out-of-the-blue signs that my work matters. For example my oddball book *Daedalus 9* is now required reading for first year students in the School of Architecture at the University of Virginia. And now your note.
Well, how could I ask for more?!!!
Yes, YOUR NOTE helps to remind me that our Mind/Soul surely is powering and storyboarding and creatively directing my life.
[And if it isn't *our* Mind and *our* Soul then whose is it? *Our* Father-Mother God: *your* Soul and *my* Soul . . . *your* Mind, *my* Mind— *everyone's* Mind/Soul. *Our* means "belonging to us"!]
Just as surely as our Mind/Soul is powering and storyboarding and creatively directing YOUR life too!!!
To make our lives add up and mean something and make a difference. And all in the service of others, ideally to help and inspire, lift up, motivate, encourage, empower, and set people free.
As so many people have done for me.

IDENTITY HEFT | 07.27.11

Today I know who I am . . .

Finally.
Go figure.

For the first time, after all these years, I now finally know the meaning of my given name—how odd that I never thought to find out and connect the dots until now.

Jeffrey = *Gift of Peace*
Hildner = *Attic Dweller*

So my name means "**Gift Of Peace, Attic Dweller**"!
I am **Gift Of Peace Who Dwells In Attic**.

Just about right for a metaphysical warrior and architect—don't you think?

And I lived for nine years at the top—in the "attic"—of a Boston brownstone.
Perfect.

I think I'm better at living up to the meaning of "attic dweller" than "gift of peace," but now that I know what's fully expected of me, maybe I'll get more in alignment with that half of my identity too!

What does your name mean?
Do you know who you are?

Sidebar: And my professional name, JEF7REY? In 1995, I learned that Piet Mondrian, the early 20th-century Dutch painter, dropped a redundant "a" from his last name: Mondriaan. And I realized that I could take similar control of my own name. So I swapped out the redundant "F" with a silent "7." Like all adopted names, my new name signifies transformation—a concept central to the spirit of a metaphysical warrior.

I AM THESEUS. So are you. The model of Theseus, the ancient Greek hero who slew the Minotaur in the Daedalus-designed Labyrinth on the island of Crete, pertains not only to the timeless outer quest for achievements and breakthroughs. The hero-model also pertains to the inner quest for enlightenment that forms and reforms our character and life-story. The outer quest—the "relentless chasing of excellence," in the words of football coach Vince Lombardi—requires fighting the monster of mediocrity, breaking free from the gravitational pull of inertia, and battling the outer gang of limitation, resistance, antagonism, revenge, and envy that tries to defeat us. The inner quest requires breaking the spell of our own inner conspirators of limitation, resistance, antagonism, revenge, and envy, and keeping discouragement, doubt, and fear at bay. On our double-quest, may we learn how to act bravely and speak gently, let in the light and explore in the dark, live in the present and outlive the past, talk straight and see around the bend, act with courage and poise but react without confusion and noise. Higher self-awareness and lower self-importance light the way through the labyrinth of outer purpose and inner identity, and like the heroes of all time who have journeyed before us, we gain enhanced capacities with every step we take.

93% of success is starting.

"We are agents of the Creative Spirit in this world. Real advance in the spiritual life means accepting this vocation with all it involves."
—Evelyn Underhill, *The Spiritual Life*

b
Mentors

The hero says, "No." The mentor says, "Go."

METAPHYSICALWARRIOR

PRIVATE

"Anything is one of a million paths. Therefore, a warrior must always keep in mind that a path is only a path; if he feels that he should not follow it, he must not stay with it under any conditions. His decision to keep on that path or to leave it must be free of fear or ambition."
—Carlos Castaneda, *The Wheel of Time*

"Attempt what is not certain." —painter Richard Diebenkorn

The slogan of the artist-pioneer! Explore *terra incognita* —unknown territory! On the other hand, my experience as an architect in the role of construction supervisor helped me craft an equally vital counter-slogan: I don't like surprises unless I know about them ahead of time.

"Mediocrity is self-inflicted and genius self-bestowed."
—philosopher Walter Russell

"Wisdom has two parts: 1) Having a lot to say. 2) Not saying it."
—church billboard in Vermont

"Never miss a good chance to shut up." —humorist Will Rogers

And yet, "What hurts the victim most is not the cruelty of the oppressor but the silence of the bystander."
—Holocaust survivor and Nobel laureate Elie Wiesel

"The hottest places in hell are reserved for those who in time of moral crisis preserve their neutrality." —Dante Alighieri

"Non-cooperation with evil is as much a moral obligation as cooperation with good." —Mahatma Gandhi

"As shells were exploding around him, he was certain that fate was keeping him safe." —History Channel program about Winston Churchill, who at 65 said, "Thus on the night of the 10th of May, at the outset of this mighty battle, I acquired the chief power in the state. At last I had the authority to give directions over the whole scene. I felt as if I were walking with destiny, and that all my past life had been but a preparation for this hour, and for this trial."

[Jesus said:] "Give your entire attention to what God is doing right now, and don't get worked up about what may or may not happen tomorrow. God will help you deal with whatever hard things come up when the time comes." —Matthew 6:34 (Eugene H. Peterson, *The Message*)

"Do not let the hero in your soul perish in lonely frustration for the life you deserve, but have never been able to reach. The world you desired can be won. It exists. It is real. It is possible. It's yours. But to win it requires your total dedication and a total break with the world of your past . . ." —John Galt, *Atlas Shrugged* by Ayn Rand

"Don't let complexity stop you." (Go around roadblocks.)
—Microsoft founder Bill Gates, Harvard Commencement 2007

"When enthusiasm encounters obstacles in the form of adverse situations or uncooperative people, it never attacks but walks around them or by yielding or embracing turns the opposing energy into a helpful one, the foe into a friend."
—Eckhart Tolle, *A New Earth*
(The word *enthusiasm* comes from Greek, meaning "god within you.")

"In a letter [Jens Peter Jacobsen] once stated his belief that every book to be of real value must embody the struggle of one or more persons against all those things which try to keep one from existing in one's own way." —O. F. Theis, Introduction to *Mogens and Other Stories* by Jens Peter Jacobsen

"The Things to do are: the things that need doing, that you see need to be done, and that no one else seems to see need to be done. Then you will conceive your own way of doing that which needs to be done—that no one else has told you to do or how to do it. This will bring out the real you that often gets buried inside a character that has acquired a superficial array of behaviors induced or imposed by others on the individual." —architect Buckminster Fuller

"Our life evokes our character and you find out more about yourself as you go on." —Joseph Campbell, *The Power of Myth*

"Break out of the concept prisons of old ideas."
—Edward de Bono, *Lateral Thinking*

"A somersault of thought into the inconceivable . . . is the act of breaking our perceptual barriers." —Carlos Castaneda, *The Power of Silence*

"Go to an extreme and then retreat to a more useful position."
—musician Brian Eno

"If you aim at nothing, you'll hit it every time."
—salesman Zig Ziglar

"You can map out a fight plan or a life plan, but when the action starts, it may not go the way you planned, and you're down to the reflexes you developed in training. That's where roadwork shows—the training you did in the dark of the mornin' will show when you're under the bright lights." —boxer Joe Frazier

"Amateurs practice until they get it right. Professionals practice until they can't get it wrong." —Unknown

"One chance is all you need." —Olympian Jesse Owens

"You can tell how big a person is by what it takes to discourage him."
—Unknown

"The mark of a certain kind of genius is the ability and energy to keep returning to the same task relentlessly, imaginatively, curiously, for a lifetime. Never give up and go onto something else; never get distracted and be diverted to something else."
—Eugene H. Peterson, *Living the Message*

"Guess what? Mistakes are gonna be made. Minimize them. Fix them. Move on. You've all had a good day." —President Josiah "Jed" Bartlet, *The West Wing*, "Mandatory Minimums" by screenwriter Aaron Sorkin

"The nerve of failure I think is paramount. Learning by mistakes. Modifying, reconstituting, reorganizing, over and over again."
—painter Wayne Thiebaud

"Fail. Fail again. Fail better." —playwright Samuel Beckett

Tracy Goss, *The Last Word on Power*—
- "I declare that I am a person who stops at nothing and I promise to allow myself to fail on any project."
- "I declare that everything needed to fulfill this possibility exists or can be created."
- POWER = "the speed with which you can declare something possible and move that possibility to reality."
- ULTIMATE POWER = "the power to get the world to match your words."
- LIFE GAME = "Making the impossible happen: freely engaging in taking risks in a game that is worth playing while life turns out the way it does."

"I think you do have to set an impossible goal. Amazing things happen when people claim responsibility for creating the impossible."
—Texas Instruments vice-president Shaunna Sowell

"One doesn't discover new lands without consenting to lose sight of the shore for a very long time." —novelist André Gide

"Be strong and courageous, and do it."
—1 Chronicles 28:20, *World English Bible*

"Counting on God's Rule to prevail, I take heart and gain strength! I run like a deer. I feel like I'm king of the mountain!"
—Habakkuk 3:19 (Eugene H. Peterson, *The Message*)

"By purifying human thought, this state of mind permeates with increased harmony all the minutiae of human affairs. It brings with it wonderful foresight, wisdom, and power; it unselfs the mortal purpose, gives steadiness to resolve, and success to endeavor."
—Mary Baker Eddy, *Miscellaneous Writings 1883-1896*

"Don't be a magician—be magic." —songwriter Leonard Cohen

"And even in our sleep pain that cannot forget falls drop by drop upon the heart, and in our own despair, against our will, comes wisdom to us by the awful grace of God." —Aeschylus

True leadership? In *Tribes: We Need You to Lead Us*, business thought-leader Seth Godin urges over-the-top underdog bravery that pushes the envelope toward a dynamic future—you've got to become the fearless "unicorn in a balloon factory" heretic who creates change with courage and guts because you believe in your tribe and its mission—
- "The desire to fail on the way to reaching a bigger goal is the untold secret of success."
- "The organizations that need innovation the most are the ones that do the most to stop it from happening."
- "If your goal is to make change, it's foolish to try to change the worldview of the majority if the majority is focused on maintaining the status quo. The opportunity is to carve out a new tribe, to find the rabble-rousers and change lovers who are seeking new leadership and run with them."
- "The secret of leadership is simple: Do what you believe in. Paint a picture of the future. Go there. People will follow."
- "Once you choose to lead, you'll be under pressure to reconsider your choice, to compromise, to dumb it down, or to give up. Of course you will. That's the world's job: to get you to be quiet and follow."

"The job of a leader is to rally people to a better future. . . . If you are going to succeed as a leader, you simply must find a way to engage our fear of the unknown and turn it into spiritedness. . . . By far the most effective way to turn fear into confidence is to be clear: to define the future in such vivid terms, through your actions, words, images, pictures, heroes, and scores that we can all see where you, and thus we, are headed. . . . Clarity is the antidote to anxiety, and therefore clarity is the preoccupation of the effective leader. If you do nothing else as a leader, be clear."
—Marcus Buckingham, *The One Thing You Need To Know*

"You don't have to know how to play the green before you tee off. You can figure it out when you get there."
—filmmaker John Sales, *City of Hope*

"What is the biggest obstacle to creativity? 'Attachment to outcome. As soon as you become attached to a specific outcome, you feel compelled to control and manipulate what you're doing. And in the process you shut yourself off to other possibilities.'"
—corporate creativity leader Gordon MacKenzie, author of *Orbiting the Giant Hairball*, from an interview in which he quipped, "Orville Wright did not have a pilot's license."

"Life's goal? Enlightenment. Practice needing nothing, but if we pursue anything it should be freedom from attachment to results."
—twitter by Russell Simmons, cofounder of Def Jam Records and author of *Super Rich*

"Freedom and happiness are found in the flexibility and ease with which we move through change." —Buddha

"I can't understand why people are frightened of new ideas. I'm frightened of the old ones." —composer John Cage

"Stop wondering whether your vision is new, / Let others make that decision . . . / They usually do! / You keep moving on."
—composer and lyricist Stephen Sondheim, "Move On," *Sunday in the Park with George*

"If you don't know where you're going, you'll end up somewhere else."
—baseball catcher Yogi Berra

"Collect yourself, let go of your ego, clear your preconceptions, and really listen. Follow your instincts and let your powerful subconscious mind guide you through the labyrinth of hidden agendas, misdirections, and half-truths."
—Derek Lin, *The Tao of Daily Life*

Trial lawyer Gerry Spence writes about "the power of listening . . . to what isn't said, to the subtext, to the iceberg of emotional truth below the surface." In other words, use your "third ear." Plus, here's what Spence says about charisma: "Charisma is the controlled transfer of raw emotion. It is getting in touch with one's own molten center and permitting it to come forth in a controlled eruption that touches the listener and passes on its inimitable heat. . . . Charisma is the transference of the passion we feel to those with whom we communicate."
—Gerry Spence, *Win Your Case*

"The skill of the persuader—the political orator, the commercial salesman, the advertiser, the propagandist—can be used with a high regard for truth and to achieve benign results, but it can also be as powerfully employed to deceive and injure. Sophistry is always a misuse of the skills of rhetoric, always an unscrupulous effort to succeed in persuading by any means, fair or foul. The line that Plato drew to distinguish the sophist from the philosopher, both equally skilled in argument, put the philosopher on the side of those who, devoted to the truth, would not misuse logic or rhetoric to win an argument by means of deception, misrepresentation, or other trickery. The sophist, in contrast, is always prepared to employ any means that will serve his purpose."
—Mortimer J. Adler, *How to Speak / How to Listen*

"Truth is powerful and it prevails."
—women's rights activist and preacher Sojourner Truth

"Joseph Campbell used to say that if you do not come to know the deeper mythic resonances that make up your life, the mythic resonances will simply rise up and take you over. If you do not live out your place in the mythic pattern consciously, the myth will simply live you against your will."
—David Whyte, *The Heart Aroused*

Joseph Campbell, *Reflections on the Art of Living*—
- "We must be willing to get rid of the life we've planned, so as to have the life that is waiting for us."
- "A bit of advice given to a young native American at the time of his initiation: As you go the way of life, you will see a great chasm. Jump. It's not as wide as you think."
- "If you follow your bliss, you put yourself on a kind of track that has been there all the while, waiting for you, and the life that you ought to be living is the one you are living. When you can see that, you begin to meet people who are in your field of bliss, and they open doors to you. I say, follow your bliss and don't be afraid, and doors will open where you didn't know they were going to be."
- "Any disaster that you can survive is an improvement in your character, your stature, and your life. What a privilege! This is when the spontaneity of your own nature will have a chance to flow. Then, when looking back at your life, you will see that the moments which seemed to be great failures followed by wreckage were the incidents that shaped the life you have now. You'll see that this is really true. Nothing can happen to you that is not positive. Even though it looks and feels at the moment like a negative crisis, it is not. The crisis throws you back, and when you are required to exhibit strength, it comes."

"The Hero embarks on the Journey and Transformation, not to gain a capacity, illumination, power or balance, but to regain it. It is not the attainment of a capacity that helps the Hero conquer his (or her) challenges but the reattainment of it."
—story designer Kal Bashir

"Each of us has a destiny. . . . What you're meant to do will follow you wherever you go."
—Victor Laszlo, *Casablanca*, by Julius J. Epstein & Philip G. Epstein (early draft of the screenplay)

"The best way to find yourself is to lose yourself in the service of others." —Mahatma Gandhi

"Everybody can be great. Because anybody can serve. You don't have to have a college degree to serve. You don't have to make your subject and your verb agree to serve. You don't have to know about Plato and Aristotle to serve. You don't have to know Einstein's theory of relativity to serve. You don't have to know the second theory of thermodynamics to serve. You only need a heart full of grace. A soul generated by love." —Dr. Martin Luther King, Jr.

"Example is not the main thing in influencing others. It's the only thing." —humanitarian Dr. Albert Schweitzer

"The practice of peace and reconciliation is one of the most vital and artistic of human actions." —Buddhist monk Thich Nhat Hanh

"Be kind, for everyone you meet is fighting a hard battle." —Plato

"I've learned that people will forget what you said, people will forget what you did, but people will never forget how you made them feel." —poet Maya Angelou

"In my younger and more vulnerable years my father gave me some advice that I've been turning over in my mind ever since. 'Whenever you feel like criticizing any one,' he told me, 'just remember that all the people in this world haven't had the advantages that you've had.'" —Nick Caraway, *The Great Gatsby* by F. Scott Fitzgerald

Dan Millman, *Wisdom of the Peaceful Warrior*—
- "Each new generation needs fresh voices to remind us of our global heritage of wisdom, in a language appropriate to each era and culture."
- "Respect and draw upon that infinite intelligence to which we all have access, if we only look, listen, and trust."
- "Be happy *now*, without reason."

"Type theory holds that the archetypes are inborn in us all. They do not have their origin in our own experience, though personal experience may activate them. They are the abstract essence of the experience and aspiration of humanity. They are the universals, the shapes of thought, which bring pattern and meaning out of the overwhelming multiplicity of life."
—Isabel Briggs Myers, *Gifts Differing*

"We are pursued by the mountains of our yesterdays, and there is no escape except on the ocean of the unknown. Yet, if we embark gladly on those dark, exhilarating waters, we find that the tide is bearing us toward horizons of morning and mountains of fulfillment we had hardly dared to imagine before this blessed catastrophe."
— Neil Millar, "The Wings of Defeat"

"In the End, we will remember not the words of our enemies, but the silence of our friends." —Dr. Martin Luther King, Jr.

"In my opinion whatever we may have to go through now is less than nothing compared with the magnificent future God has planned for us. The whole creation is on tiptoe to see the wonderful sight of the sons of God coming into their own."
—Romans 8:18-19, J.B. Phillips, *New Testament in Modern English*

"How could we be capable of forgetting the old myths that stand at the threshold of all mankind, myths of dragons transforming themselves at the last moment into princesses? Perhaps all dragons in our lives are really princesses just waiting to see us just once being beautiful and courageous." —Rainer Maria Rilke, *Letters to a Young Poet*

"We must learn that evil is the awful deception and unreality of existence. Evil is not supreme; good is not helpless; nor are the so-called laws of matter primary, and the law of Spirit secondary."
—Mary Baker Eddy, *Science and Health*

"Talent is luck. The important thing in life is courage."
—filmmaker Woody Allen, *Manhattan*

"The adventure is always and everywhere a passage beyond the veil of the known; the powers that watch at the boundary are dangerous; to deal with them is risky; yet for anyone with competence and courage the danger fades."
—Joseph Campbell, *The Hero with a Thousand Faces*

"My earliest mentor, W. Clement Stone, was once described as an inverse paranoid. Instead of believing the world was plotting to do him harm, he chose to believe the world was plotting to do him good. Instead of seeing every difficult or challenging event as a negative, he saw it for what it could be—something that was meant to enrich him, empower him, or advance his causes. What an incredibly positive belief! Imagine how much easier it would be to succeed in life if you were constantly expecting the world to support you and bring you opportunity. Successful people do just that." —Jack Canfield, *The Success Principles*

"In your own life, what barriers are waiting to be defied? . . . The history books are written about those who defy, not conform. Give your own situation a careful examination and choose the areas of your life most in need of disruption. Defy the norm. Defy the obvious. Defy the expected. Defy the critics. Defy your boundaries and seize the life you were meant to live." —entrepreneur Josh Linkner

"Creative work is not a selfish act or a bid for attention on the part of the actor. It's a gift to the world and every being in it. Don't cheat us of your contribution. Give us what you got."
—Steven Pressfield, *The War of Art*

13 FAVORITE BIBLE VERSES (*King James Version*):

1. Exodus 23:20—"Behold, I send an Angel before thee, to keep thee in the way, and to bring thee into the place which I have prepared."
2. Job 11:17—"And thine age shall be clearer than the noonday; thou shalt shine forth, thou shalt be as the morning."
3. Job 28:23—"God understandeth the way thereof, and he knoweth the place thereof."
4. Job 33:4—"The spirit of God hath made me, and the breath of the Almighty hath given me life."
5. Psalms 1:3—"And he shall be like a tree planted by the rivers of water, that bringeth forth his fruit in his season; his leaf also shall not wither; and whatsoever he doeth shall prosper."
6. Psalms 71:1—"In thee, O Lord, do I put my trust; let me never be put to confusion."
7. Psalms 91:10,11—"There shall no evil befall thee; neither shall any plague come nigh thy dwelling. For he shall give his angels charge over thee to keep thee [safe, whole, fruitful] in all thy ways."
8. Proverbs 3:5,6—"Trust in the Lord with all thine heart; and lean not unto thine own understanding. In all thy ways acknowledge him, and he shall direct thy paths."
9. Isaiah 41:10—"Fear thou not; for I am with thee: be not dismayed; for I am thy God: I will strengthen thee; yea, I will help thee; yea, I will uphold thee with the right hand of my righteousness."
10. Isaiah 58:11—"And the Lord shall guide thee continually, and satisfy thy soul in drought, and make fat thy bones: and thou shalt be like a watered garden, and like a spring of water, whose waters fail not."
11. Jeremiah 29:11—"For I know the thoughts that I think toward you, saith the Lord, thoughts of peace, and not of evil, to give you an expected end." ("'For I know the plans I have for you,' declares the Lord, 'plans to prosper you and not to harm you, plans to give you hope and a future.'" —*New International Bible*)
12. Zephaniah 3:17—"The LORD thy God in the midst of thee is mighty; he will save, he will rejoice over thee with joy; he will rest in his love, he will joy over thee with singing."
13. Revelation 3:8—"I know thy works: behold, I have set before thee an open door, and no man can shut it . . ."

[Competence +

COURAGE Eyr 23:20   Jeffrey

BE THOU strong and very courageous. It is foolish and sinful to doubt the goodness and power of God. All of good is everywhere, never divided nor limited, and enough for all. We must have strength, courage, and faith to trust God always and all the way. Divine Love is the only power and presence of the universe, here, now, and you can not be shut out from His joy. The promise and fulfilment go hand in hand, and now is the day of salvation from all unlike good. Our understanding of God must equal our faith in Him; then we are intelligently praying, and the result is certain and sure. The argument that would discourage is not born of the Father, is not supported by law, hence it is baseless and base.

Be strong, dear heart. Live one day at the time. Yesterday never was—tomorrow never will be; there is no time but now. And by doing our intelligent best today, tomorrow brings another day in which we can know more and more of Him from whom all blessings flow. Be cheerful. Hope all things, endure all things, expect all good to come, and come soon, and, as we deserve it, God will make it so. Be strong and of good courage.

—Edward Everett Norwood

Source unknown.

I HAVE THE COMPETENCE + COURAGE TO DO WHAT NEEDS TO BE DONE TO DO WHAT'S RIGHT — TO PASS ALL THE HEROES TESTS

I AM STRONG AND OF GOOD COURAGE

I "EXPECT ALL GOOD TO COME AND COME SOON"

Δ

"Let me tell ya somethin' ya already know... You, me, or nobody is gonna hit as hard as life. But it ain't how hard ya hit. It's about how hard ya can get hit, and keep moving forward."
—Rocky, *Rocky Balboa*, by Sylvester Stallone

EXPECT GOOD BEYOND MEASURE TO APPEAR IN YOUR LIFE TODAY. **EXPECT TANGIBLE PROOF OF THIS TRUTH:**
PSALMS 23: 6—
"SURELY GOODNESS AND MERCY SHALL FOLLOW ME ALL THE DAYS OF MY LIFE."
AND I WILL DWELL IN THE HOUSE OF THE METAPHYSICAL WARRIOR FOREVER.

Frank Bold-Write, Architect

A few backstage notes about word building.

I want to pull back the curtain and reveal some notes about writing mainly for two reasons: 1) I respect the professional demands of the writer's craft, and 2) This book may give little proof of that, so these notes can at least attest to my tries.

GREAT MUSICIANS ARE LIKE GREAT FIGHTERS. THEY HAVE A HIGHER SENSE OF THEORY GOING ON IN THEIR HEADS. —Miles Davis

I said in an earlier chapter that to me, writing feels like painting. But I'm not only a painter, I'm also an architect, so to me, writing also feels like designing a building. In my world, an essay or a book, no less than a wall or a house, if well crafted, amounts to a practical and poetic expression of form and content, technique and imagination, control and soul. And to hone my design skills as a writer, I surf the waves that rise from the ocean depths of theory. Because as jazz legend Miles Davis said about great fighters and great musicians, great writers (like great painters and great architects) "have a higher sense of theory going on in their heads."

I've learned that making deft and creative choices about the contours of words and sentences, paragraphs and pages, setups and payoffs, while turning thoughts into the music of language, requires not only a higher sense of theory. The pursuit of great writing also requires grit: mental toughness and courage in the face of uncompromising self-criticism.

Listen to story wizard Robert McKee explain what separates professionals from amateurs: "Amateurs love everything they write. . . . Professionals hate everything they write. They destroy their work in pursuit of excellence, because they have high standards. . . . You have to be ruthless toward your own writing."

On their quest to make their work first-rate, professionals write and rewrite, tossing 93% of what they create. They won't quit till they find some semblance of the mediocre-free 7% worth printing.

I taught myself a lot about the theory and professional practice of writing during the nine years that I worked for weekly and monthly magazines published by The Christian Science Publishing Society (CSPS). A line by Mary Baker Eddy, the founder of these magazines, reminds me to know my audience. In a letter to one of her students, Eddy wrote, "We must write more for the people who know not C.S. than for [the] mass who do" (L11048, John F. Linscott, June 8, 1897). Because of that line, I try to hit the delete key on jargon. No insider language. Whether I write about metaphysics or architecture or painting, I use familiar words to convey unfamiliar concepts. I use simple language to convey complex ideas.

I follow Gary Provost's advice in *100 Ways to Improve Your Writing*: "Use short words instead of long ones. Don't write like a Scrabble champion."

Motivational speaker Zig Ziglar said, "If you aim at nothing, you hit it every time." Or as they say in football and hockey, you can't score without a goal. So another one of my goals as a writer, as Kurt Vonnegut put it: "You've got to be a good date for the reader." How? Screenwriter Max Adams gives this advice, "The only real rule I know in writing is, *Don't be boring*." To which I would add, "Give your date an easy read." But heads up: An easy read requires hard work. As Nathaniel Hawthorne confessed, "Easy reading makes damn hard writing." Yes, professionals knuckle down to find that 7%—so they can be a good date for the reader.

My go-to books on writing? The ones I rely on most to gain a higher sense of theory and to help me master the craft? *A Writer's Coach* by Jack Hart and *Writing Tools* by Roy Peter Clark. I've learned more about the principles of good writing from these two books than I learned from any course I took as an undergraduate and graduate student at Princeton.

My education as a writer started in 1990, nine years after I got my master's degree in architecture. I worked with Nora Odendahl, then editor of *Architecture New Jersey*, to shipshape my essay "Drawing as Contemplation" for publication. Nora explained when to use *that* and when to use *which*. She helped me get my sentences under control without sacrificing their soul. She showed me how to close the gap between expressing ideas in ways that made sense to me and expressing ideas in ways that would make sense to my reader. Nora was the first to school me in how to write with my reader in mind: simply and clearly.

Jump to 1998. My education went up a notch or three when I wrote non-bylined articles about spirituality for *The Christian Science Monitor*. I got lots of practice in the art of writing to word count. (Why did my high school and college teachers, and my daughter's too, ask us to count pages instead of words?) I taught myself how to construct a journalism-standard 700- to 750-word essay. Before working full-time for CSPS, I wrote 41 of those freelance essays, and when I joined the staff, my skill set served me well, especially as a non-bylined editorial writer for the *Christian Science Sentinel* during my last two years on the job—again, writing to a tight word count.

During those crucial formative years from 1998-2001, *Language in Thought and Action* by S.I. Hayakawa (a writing-theory rock) encouraged me to nimbly slide up and down the ladder of abstraction and make a lot of what I say concrete: Say something I can point to, like that palm tree outside my window.

So I learned to *make writing visual*. And in turn, I learned to make reading visual—in more ways than one, as H. W. Fowler's *Modern English Usage* gets across: "Paragraphing is also a matter of the eye. A reader will address himself more readily to his task if he sees from the start that he will have breathing-spaces from time to time than if what is before him looks like a marathon course." So at the end of every paragraph, like this one, I try to leave lots of white space.

This space not only makes the look and feel of the text more reader friendly, this space also amplifies the most important word-choice in a paragraph: the last word.

Oh, and the most important word in a sentence? The last word. Thanks to Roy Peter Clark, I see myself on a balance beam. Because a writer is a gymnast, and you gotta stick the landing.

Walter Fox's *Writing the News* taught me to swap multi-syllable Latin words for short Anglo-Saxon words. "Most short English words," writes Fox, "—such as 'home,' 'friend,' 'land' and 'drunk'—are of Anglo-Saxon origin. These words resonate with greater emotional power than their equivalents in Latin derivation—which in the above case, would be 'domicile,' 'acquaintance,' 'nation' and 'inebriated.' In addition to being long, Latin-root words tend to be abstract and emotionally detached in contrast to the strong, vigorous, Anglo-Saxon vocabulary."

In *Why I Write,* George Orwell coached me to follow the same principle: "Bad writers . . . are nearly always haunted by the notion that Latin or Greek words are grander than Saxon ones." On page 177, I list Orwell's six good-writer rules.

I wish I could recall who said that amateurs don't have a style—only professionals have a style. E.B. White, author of *The Elements of Style*, defined style as "the sound words make on paper." Brooks Landon, author of *Building Great Sentences*, writes that "one of the functions of style [is] to remind us of the mind behind the sentences we read."

"Whether short or long," writes Landon, "sentences are the

most important building blocks of prose, the foundation of written communication, and always the essential units of prose style."

What do we read? Sentences. Sentences can roll and flow. They can stop. And they can go—take the local or the express and either hurry or delay. Sentences can work or play. They can go short. Or they can go long, revealing or concealing, disclosing or withholding, telling or showing, zigzagging or tightroping ahead as they post information for our edification (oops, sorry about that fancy Latin-based word) and move us through their patterns and sounds that strike us as either pretty or gritty.

Or witty.

Sentences are the melodic line of a writer's music. Words are the notes. And good writers read their work aloud to hear how it sounds to a reader. As Jack Hart reports in *A Writer's Coach*, good writers move their lips as they type.

Novelist Don DeLillo: "There's a rhythm I hear that drives me through a sentence. And the words typed on the white page have a sculptural quality. They form odd correspondences. They match up not just through meaning but through sound and look. The rhythm of a sentence will accommodate a certain number of syllables. One syllable too many, I look for another word. There's always another word that means nearly the same thing, and if it doesn't then I'll consider altering the meaning of a sentence to keep the rhythm, the syllable beat. I'm completely willing to let language press meaning upon me. Watching the way in which words match up, keeping the balance in a sentence—these are sensuous pleasures."

Did you read all of that? If not, you might chalk it up to my breaking novelist Elmer Leonard's 10th rule of writing: "Try to leave out the part that readers tend to skip." (No offence, Don! I love every word.)

Think of writing as a gold coin. On one side: Function. On the flip side: Form. And like DeLillo, Orwell reassures me that great writers—like great architects—don't treasure function more than form. Orwell said, "I could not do the work of writing a book or even a long magazine article, if it were not also an aesthetic experience."

BTW, that riff above by DeLillo? He starts it with this line: "This is what I mean when I call myself a writer. I construct sentences."

Beautiful. Me too.

PRINCIPLES AT WORK

Architect Frank Lloyd Wright said, "Don't go into architecture to get a living unless you love it as a principle at work."

And likewise, I say, "Don't become a writer unless you love writing as a system of principles at work."

At the top of my checklist of principles, I keep these three words inspired by Michelangelo: Free The Angel.

And under those three words, I keep the quotations sprinkled through this essay, as well as reminders such as these:

MAKE IT VISUAL. Paint word pictures. ("Make 'em see what you're saying." —*Pop!: Stand Out in Any Crowd* by Sam Horn)

Paint the canvas with FACTS, SYMBOLS, and EMOTIONS.
Remember actor John Lithgow's insight. Words operate at three levels:
   MEANING, MUSIC, and EMOTION.
Remember Aristotle: BEGINNING, MIDDLE, END.

KNOW YOUR AUDIENCE—Your readers expect you to engage them in four basic ways: DATA, STRUCTURE, VISION, and HUMANITY. The component of "humanity" answers the reader's question, "What's in it for me?"
(See "Speaking in Tongues," by David Wagner, *MIT Sloan Management Review*, July 1, 2006.)

"Let it flow, without criticizing it too close to its creation."
—educator Anne Carroll Moore

"Blend the serious with the humorous without disgrace."
—art historian Marilyn Lavin

"All styles are good, except the boring." —Voltaire

Give your sentence a spring. "It's got to have this little spring."
—novelist and screenwriter Ian McEwan, commenting on novelist John Updike's requirement for a sentence

"I see but one rule: to be clear." —Stendahl

"As a reader, I want a book to kidnap me into its world."
—novelist and poet Erica Jong

"To get to the truth, get your own heart to pound while you write."
—story guru Robert McKee

George Orwell's rules (*Why I Write*):
i. Never use a metaphor, simile, or other figure of speech which you are used to seeing in print.
ii. Never use a long word where a short one will do.
iii. If it is possible to cut a word out, always cut it out.
iv. Never use the passive where you can use the active.
v. Never use a foreign phrase, a scientific word, or a jargon word if you can think of an everyday English equivalent.
vi. Break any of these rules sooner than say anything outright barbarous.

"The secret of all writing is to make every word count."
—pulp fiction author Lester Dent

"BLEND CONTROL AND SOUL. Develop your project with the layered honesty, conscientious detail, contrapuntal and polyphonic depth, and crystal clarity of a Bach fugue, O musical one! Write from the depths of your unique being. Stay open to insight and wit. Trust the interplay of analysis and intuition, nerd and free spirit. Mix cool reason with creative fire!"
—Frank Bold-Write, Architect

My checklist includes many more guiding principles. Roy Peter Clark taught me, for example, how to rank a sequence of three: 2, 3, 1. Illustration: Three more keys to my writing? Use active verbs instead of the amateur writer's sentence-deflating and lazy go-to verb *is*, rely on Flesch-Kincaid grade level and reading ease tests, and write the end first.

WRITING IS ARCHITECTURE

Le Corbusier, the great 20th-century Swiss-French architect, observed, "Everything is architecture." True. In everything I see and everything I can't see, I look for some unifying and coherent blueprint or form. And I find that so much in life imitates a building and involves the structure of aesthetic, pragmatic, and symbolic relationships and expresses a system of principles at work. This applies to everything from the sun and its planets to a sports team, a supermarket, a movie, or a marriage—from human experience to metaphysical reality. From a sentence to a book.

So why do I write? To define the architecture of the world. To redesign the world. And in the words of Irish poet Seamus Heaney, I write "to see myself, to set the darkness echoing."

MEACAIM

Say "yes" to the herald-call inviting you to become a metaphysical warrior, and watch your life go from black and white to technicolor.

HEADS UP:
Just before you break through the sound barrier is when the cockpit shakes the most.
—test pilot Chuck Yeager

Metadata

Bibliography and recommended books.

BIBLIOGRAPHY:

Since 1998, I've written more than 200 articles on spiritual themes for the periodicals and websites of The Christian Science Publishing Society. Ranging from 500 to 5,000 words, these articles include essays, interviews, profiles, and editorials, as well as special-feature commentaries and reviews of movies and books.

I used the phrase "metaphysical warrior" for the first time in an article that appeared in the July 2009 issue of *The Christian Science Journal*: "Christian Healing: Field-Tested Insights—A Conversation With Jim Spencer" (pp. 22-28). On page 24, I said, "And I've found that if you don't want evil—even the illusion of evil—to harm you, then you have to wage a fierce mental battle. You have to be a metaphysical warrior."

In my unsigned editorial "Bounce Back" for the *Christian Science Sentinel* (June 28, 2010, p. 28), I first quoted Mary Baker Eddy's line that I've adopted as a core slogan of the metaphysical warrior (*Science and Health*, p. 419): "Meet every adverse circumstance as its master."

Then in my last on-staff article, I folded Eddy's underappreciated seven-word imperative into a bylined *Sentinel* three-pager (December 5, 2011, pp. 6-8) that I headlined, "Free the angel."

Not counting republication of articles in other languages in the *Herald of Christian Science*, the following represents a fairly complete list of my articles through 2011. Starting in mid-2004, when my role as senior writer/editor for the *Sentinel* and *Journal* expanded to include creative director for the two magazines, I also designed the layout of my articles, often including original artwork and photographs to help tell the story. You can find the text of many articles online.

The Christian Science Journal
(CSB = Christian Science teacher)
"Mortal, human, divine," CSB interview, photo, and layout; September 2011, pp. 14-21.
"Life . . . and life," CSB interview and layout; May 2011, pp. 18-25.
"Through the lens of God's Science," CSB interview and layout; February 2011, pp. 20-26.
"In *real* Science we trust," CSB interview and layout; December 2010, pp. 20-26.
"When justice and affection blend," CSB interview and layout; October 2010, pp. 20-26.
"CS 360," CSB interview and layout; August 2010, pp. 24-30.
"Practical Science," CSB interview and layout; May 2010, pp. 20-27.
"Thought paint," CSB interview and layout; April 2010, pp. 22-29.
"Not guilty," CSB interview and layout; February 2010, pp. 20-26.
"The self-acting power of CS," CSB interview and layout; December 2009, pp. 22-28.

"Sing gratitude's refrain" (aka "Horizon Lines"), poem/sonnet, layout, and excerpt from my painting *Harbor*; November 2009, p. 57.
"Stability you can count on," CSB interview and layout; September 2009, pp. 22-28.
"Outlook Nigeria: a correct view," CSB interview and layout; August 2009, pp. 20-26.
"Christian healing: field-tested insights," CSB interview, photos, and layout; July 2009, pp. 22-29.
"Good's infinite embrace," CSB interview and layout; June 2009, pp. 22-29.
"Inner architecture," profile of architect Gabriela Meyer, photo, and layout; May 2009, pp. 54-57.
"The Science and art of Christian healing," CSB interview and layout; March 2009, pp. 20-27.
"Always an answer," CSB interview and layout; February 2009, pp. 20-27.
"The Virginian," interview of actor Robert Duvall, photos, and layout; December 2008, pp. 50-55.
"Healing rules," CSB interview and layout; November 2008, pp. 18-25.
"The great rhythms of Life," CSB interview and layout; October 2008, pp. 18-25.
"What in the world are Christian Science Reading Rooms?" August 2008, pp. 45+.*
"Intelligence now," cover story, illustrations, and layout, July 2008, pp. 32-38.
"Journey to healing," CSB interview and layout; May 2008, pp. 18-25.
"Everyone deserves healing," CSB interview and layout; March 2008, pp. 18-25.
"Put God first," CSB interview and layout; January 2008, pp. 18-25.
"Future fuel unlimited," interview of physicist Michael Antal, photo, and layout; June 2008, pp. 54-57.
"Soular power," cover story, interviews, and layout; February 2008, pp. 36-48.
"Spiritual medicine," CSB interview and layout; November 2007, pp. 18-25.
"God rules," CSB interview and layout; October 2007, pp. 18-25.
"Church fuel," CSB interview and layout; September 2007, pp. 18-25.
"Inner vision," CSB interview and layout; August 2007, pp. 16-23.
"Riches of the Spirit," CSB interview, photo, and layout; June 2007, pp. 14-21.
"This simple rule," essay, layout, and my painting *topo|Markings_4* (aka *Troy*), May 2007, pp. 62-63.
"Healthy planet/green planet: global warming and prayer," cover story and layout; April 2007, pp. 46-51.
"Fundamentals on the lacrosse field of life," profile of Theresa Sherry; March 2007, pp. 50-51.
"Powered by Love," CSB interview, photos, and layout; February 2007, pp. 14-21.
"Square One: Journal cover 2007," commentary; January 2007, p. 5.
"Make people think," CSB interview, photos, and layout; December 2006, pp. 14-21.
"Practical Science: geometry lessons," profile of mathematician Frank Morgan, photos, and layout; October 2006, pp. 52-55.
"Christ Love," CSB interview and layout; August 2006, pp. 16-23 (ends with painting by Richard Diebenkorn: *Ocean Park No. 107*, 1978).
"Everlasting grace," interview of dramatist and screenwriter Horton Foote, photo, and layout; July 2006, pp. 34-39.
"The majesty of Christian Science," cover-story essay, interviews, and layout; June 2006, pp. 38-53.
"A call to the chaplaincy," May 2006, pp. 16-19.
"Total income," interview of artist Brooks Anderson and layout; April 2006, pp. 40-45.
"Higher love," CSB interview, layout, and photo of Nairobi; March 2006, pp. 16-23.

"Road to Nairobi . . . and back (changed)," article, photos, and layout (including photos by my daughter, Emily Madison Hildner); February 2006, pp. 36-45.
"Soul thinking," CSB interview and layout; January 2006, pp. 20-27.*
"Stay open," December 2005, pp. 16+.*
"Bible language—Now!" December 2005, pp. 13+.*
"True identity," CSB interview and layout; November 2005, pp. 24-31 (ends with painting by Richard Diebenkorn: *Woman in Profile*, 1958).
"Chain reaction," essay, photo, and layout; November 2005, p. 64.
"Disarming ignorance and malice," October 2005, pp. 16-19.
"Healing light," CSB interview and layout; August 2005, pp. 20-25.
"Time, space, matter: seeing through the grand illusion," cover-story essay, interviews (including physicist Brian Greene), photos, and layout; July 2005, pp. 44-55.
"Square one," commentary; June 2005, p. 7.
"Natural humility," CSB interview and layout; May 2005, pp. 16-23.*
"Like breathing," CSB interview and layout; April 2005, pp. 16-23 (ends with painting by Richard Diebenkorn: *Figure on a Porch*, 1959).
"Believe God," CSB interview and layout (including photos by my daughter, Emily Madison Hildner); March 2005, pp. 20-27.
"Through a unique lens," February 2005, pp. 38-51.
"Science of being enters the academic arena," January 2005, pp. 42+.*
"Walking the path," CSB interview; January 2005, pp. 18-25.*
"Prayer power," CSB interview and layout; December 2004, pp. 28-33.
"Advancing public access to spiritual healing in the information age," December 2004, pp. 14-27.
"The big picture," CSB interview and photo; November 2004, pp. 30-37.*
"Public speaking for a spiritually hungry world," November 2004, pp. 15+.*
"Wake up to individuality," CSB interview; October 2004, pp. 30-35.
"Spiritual education for children," October 2004, pp. 12-29.
"Spiritual healing," CSB interview; August 2004, pp. 36-39.*
"Growing a church for the ages: a blueprint for action," August 2004, pp. 19+.*
"Spiritual healing," CSB interview; July 2004, pp. 34-37.*
"Healing messages for everyday study and Sunday sermons," July 2004, pp. 18-33.
"The power of unselfish love," book review and interview of Stephen Post, author of *Unlimited Love: Altruism, Compassion, and Service*; June 2004, pp. 54-56.
"Remarkable innovation in moving a message outward," June 2004, pp. 16-31.
"Spiritual healing," CSB interview; May 2004, pp. 31-33.*
"Journalism for a spiritual age," May 2004, pp. 15-28.*
"Spiritual healing," CSB interview; April 2004, pp. 30-33.*
"Church services for a global community," April 2004, pp. 16-29.
"Truth and modern dance?" profile of dancer David Grenke, March 2004, pp. 44-46.
"Spiritual healing," CSB interview; March 2004, pp. 30-33.
"A course in metaphysical healing," March 2004, pp. 16-24.
"Spiritual healing," CSB interview; February 2004, pp. 32-35.
"Restoring and forwarding Christian healing," February 2004, pp. 20-28.
"What do you find when you road trip through America's religious landscape?" book review and interview of Tom Levinson, author of *All That's Holy*; January 2004, pp. 34-35.
"Spiritual healing," CSB interview; January 2004, pp. 22-25.
"*Science and Health*: The book that launched a global movement," January 2004, pp. 14-21.
"Spiritual healing," CSB interview; December 2003, pp. 20-23.

"Give/give = win/win," December 2003, pp. 9-10.
"Experiencing the 'click' of recognition that God is here," book review of *The God of Old: Inside the Lost World of the Bible* by James L. Kugel; November 2003, pp. 44-45.
"Spiritual healing," CSB interview; November 2003, pp. 20-23.
"Destination: healing," November 2003, pp. 6-9.
"In the hills and valleys—God is there," book review of *Strength for the Journey: Biblical Wisdom for Daily Living* by Peter J. Gomes; October 2003, pp. 28-29.
"Spiritual healing," CSB interview; October 2003, pp. 20-23.
"An echo through the universe," September 2003, p. 5.
"Let in the light," book review of *God's Secretaries: The Making of the King James Bible* by Adam Nicolson; August 2003, pp. 54-55.
"Unity and joy in Boston," August 2003, pp. 40-42.
"Spiritual healing," CSB interview; August 2003, pp. 18-21.
"Learning that God's guidance is always at hand," part 3 of 3; July 2003, pp. 44-46.
"Spiritual Healing," CSB interview; July 2003, pp. 29-31.
"Three brothers, jobs, and prayer," July 2003, pp. 9-11.
"A Bible-based view of wealth: Is it practical today?" book review of *Faithful Finances 101* by Gary Moore; July 2003, pp. 10-11.
"X-ing out terrorism—a call to redouble global prayer," book review of *The Crisis of Islam: Holy War and Unholy Terror* by Bernard Lewis; June 2003, pp. 58-59.
"Learning that God's guidance is always at hand," part 2 of 3; June 2003, pp. 52-53.
"From Salt Lake to Rome—the global chain of spiritual awakening," June 2003, p. 43.
"United in a quest to end suffering (through a change of thought)," June 2003, pp. 42-43.
"Learning that God's guidance is always at hand," part 1 of 3, May 2003, pp. 40-42.
"A parent's prayer," commentary; May 2003, p. 5.
"Bringing calm to work—and beyond," April 2003, pp. 34-35.
"Spiritual healing," CSB interview and my painting *Infinity* (aka *Aeneas*); April 2003, pp. 18-22.
"Proactive prayer to overcome poverty and racism," interview of Jim Wallis; March 2003, pp. 42-43.
"Breaking free from unwritten rules," book review of *Who Says Elephants Can't Dance: Inside IBM's Historic Turnaround* by Louis V. Gerstner, Jr.; March 2003, pp. 37/49.
"Forgiveness heals, data shows," March 2003, p. 19.
"Want healing? Let go of that grudge," March 2003, pp. 18-19.
"Drums of healing," interview of Babatunde Olatunji; February 2003, pp. 32-33.
"Helping people find the Divine," book review of *Wisdom Bowls: Overcoming Fear and Coming Home to Your Authentic Self* by Meredith Young-Sowers; January 2003, p. 60.
"What *Science and Health* says about evolution," January 2003, pp. 46-47.
"A world of ideas," December 2002, pp. 50-53.
"Profile: Spirituality & Health magazine," interview of editor Robert Own Scott; December 2002, pp. 46-47.
"A global impulse for good," interviews; November 2002, pp. 46-47.
"Regular giving helps good things happen," November 2002, pp. 44-45.
"Prayer from Ground Zero on September 11, 2002," November 2002, p. 15.
"The power of the word—spoken and written," October 2002, p. 44.
"Live events make connections," interviews; October 2002, pp. 41-44.
"A design tradition of simplicity and excellence," interview of architect Ann Beha; September 2002, pp. 29-31.
"Midnight moments break into light," commentary; September 2002, p. 5.
"Boats may be safe in the harbor, but . . . ," commentary; April 2002, p. 5.

"Green Pastures," October 2001, p. 35.
"Spirituality and the need for structure," book review of *Why Religion Matters: The Fate of the Human Spirit in an Age of Disbelief* by Huston Smith; September 2001, p. 15.
"Engaging with deep things in the universe," September 2009, pp. 12-14.
"Not just another Whitman's sampler," book and movie review of *Chocolate* by Joanne Harris—screenplay by Robert Nelson Jacobs; June 2001, pp. 44-45.

Christian Science Sentinel

"Free the angel," lead article for the issue "Art & Soul," layout, and my painting *Icarus*; December 5, 2011, pp. 6-8.
"The forever flow-motion of good," editorial; November 7, 2011, p. 28.
"Progress in process," editorial; October 10, 2011, p. 28.
"Be one of those," editorial; August 29, 2011, p. 28.
"Your divine 'Career Counselor,'" editorial; July 18, 2011, p. 28.
"Perception management," editorial; June 6, 2011, p. 28.
"Deliver a mental knockout punch to fraud," editorial; May 2, 2011, p. 28.
"Turn here," editorial; March 8, 2011, p. 28.
"What do we cling to," editorial; February 21, 2011, p. 28.
"Righteous rebellion," editorial; January 10, 2011, p. 28.
"Movie business," editorial; December 6, 2010, p. 28.
"F.E.A.R.," editorial; October 25, 2010, p. 28.
"Wide-angle view," editorial; September 20, 2010, p. 28.
"Spirit visible," editorial; August 9, 2010, p. 28.
"Bounce back," editorial; June 28, 2010, p. 28.
"Mind unlimited," editorial; May 17, 2010, p. 28.
"Earthquake resistant prayers," editorial; April 12, 2010, p. 28.
"Love your enemies," editorial; March 8, 2010, p. 28.
"'Send now prosperity'," editorial; February 1, 2010, p. 28.
"Hope," prose-poem and layout; January 18 & 25, 2010, p. 19.
"On the season of origins," editorial; December 21, 2009, p. 27.
"Time masters," cover-story roundtable and layout; August 3, 2009, pp. 6-9.
"Flight plan," article and layout; May 18, 2009, p. 13.
"Look anew: what do you see?" essay, photo, and layout; July 21 & 28, 2008, pp. 22-23.
"39 across," essay, photo, and layout; January 14 & 21, 2008, pp. 26-27.
"Sign language," essay, photo, and layout; July 23 & 30, 2007, pp. 28-29.
"Light ribbons/Manhattan skyline," essay, photo, and layout; July 24 & 31, 2006, pp. 34-35.
"Rest," essay, photo, and layout; November 14, 2005, p. 21.
"$E=mc^2$ but . . . $H=de^n$ " (Healing = divine energy, now!), commentary; July 11, 2005, p. 3.
"Make poverty history," movie review of *The Constant Gardener*; November 7, 2005, p. 21.
"Arrangement in red and gray," essay, photo, and layout; May 16, 2005, p. 21.
"The message is YES!" with Marilyn Jones, article and layout; November 29, 2004, pp. 6-9.
"'Go see Mike,'" article, photos, and layout; July 12, 2004, pp. 12-15.
"'Everybody can be great,'" article and photos; February 16, 2004, pp. 18-19.
"Flight forces," article (first time I contributed design decisions: the color display type that threads through the article); December 1, 2003, pp. 16-17.
"Divine 'lightning bolts' strike every heart," article; June 23, 2003, pp. 14-15.
"Inspiration from a spelling bee," article; August 5, 2002, pp. 18-19.
"Heroes and light in NYC," article; December 3, 2001, pp. 18-19.

"Shrek: What's Love Got To Do With It?" movie review of *Shrek*; August 13, 2001, pp. 22-23.
"There's a whale waiting," article; August 6, 2001, pp. 22-23.
"Say 'no' to worry," article and visuals; April 2, 2001, pp. 16-17.
"Why we're here," article reprinted from *The Christian Science Monitor*; November 27, 2000, p. 9.

Additional Artwork and Photos (not associated with above TCSJ and CSS articles)
Ulysses, excerpt of painting; *TCSJ*, November 2010, cover and cover story, pp. 34-35.
Seaport, excerpt of painting; *TCSJ*, April 2010, cover and cover story, p. 30.
Ithaca, excerpt of painting; *TCSJ*, January 2010, cover.
Harbor, excerpt of painting; *CSS*, August 3, 2009, p. 15.
Waterfall [aka *Mariner*], painting; *TCSJ*, October 2007, pp. 18-25.
"Closet prayer," cartoon (writer and designer) with Joy Cusak; *TCSJ*, December 2007, p. 57.
"Swap Seats," cartoon (writer and designer) with Joy Cusak; *TCSJ*, July 2007, p. 63.
"Listening," cartoon (writer and designer) with Joy Cusak; *TCSJ*, June 2007, p. 63.
"Still Waters—Little Pleasant Bay," photo; *TCSJ*, June 2007, p. 23.
deep edge _11 / landscape and window [aka *Labyrinth*], painting; *TCSJ*, January 2007, pp. 22-23.
"Hotel Nairobi," photo; *CSS*, January 1, 2007, p. 11.
Abstract Field -3 [aka *Aeneas*], excerpt of painting; *TCSJ*, March 2005, cover and pp. 46-47.

Christian Science Sentinel—Radio Edition
"Living in the now," August 1, 2009; Program 931.
"Decision-making, with help from that 'still, small voice'," March 20, 2004; Program 30-412.
"When walls come down," 2004; Program 326.
"Useful ideas for today's parents," taped December 15, 2000; Program 05.
"Rewarding Careers," taped March 28, 2000; Program 028.

spirituality.com (pre-2002) (These articles no longer appear online.)
"A parent's prayer in a threatening situation," November 18, 2001.
"Well able is Allah to save," September 21, 2001.
"Seeking spirituality in NYC," May 23, 2001.
"Walk worthy," May 7, 2001.
"Oscar® light," April 9, 2001.
"A good, honourable, and brave career," April 6, 2001.
"The similarities of spiritual seekers," November 30, 2000.

The Christian Science Monitor
Except where noted, these 750-word articles appeared originally in the print version of the newspaper and can be read online at www.csmonitor.com.
"F.E.A.R.," October 25, 2010
  www.csmonitor.com/The-Culture/Articles-on-Christian-Science/2010/1025/F.E.A.R
  (first published in the *Christian Science Sentinel*, Ocober 25, 2010, p. 28)
"'Send now prosperity': a response to unemployment," February 3, 2010
  www.csmonitor.com/The-Culture/Articles-on-Christian-Science/2010/0203/Send-now-prosperity-a-response-to-unemployment
  (first published in the *Christian Science Sentinel*, February 1, 2010, p. 2)
"Seven words," December 1, 2003 www.csmonitor.com/2003/1201/p18s01-hfcs.html
"Central Park lessons," May 29, 2003 www.csmonitor.com/2003/0529/p18s01-hfcs.html
"Mental architecture," July 10, 2002 www.csmonitor.com/2002/0710/p18s01-hfcs.html

"Our forever Father," June 14, 2002 www.csmonitor.com/2002/0614/p22s01-hfcs.html
"An unhurried year ahead," December 27, 2001 www.csmonitor.com/2001/1227/p19s1-hfcs.html
"Career construction and the art of airplane design," June 25, 2001
    www.csmonitor.com/2001/0625/p19s1.html
"Commencement—it's just the beginning," June 12, 2001 www.csmonitor.com/2001/0612/p19s1.html
"Waves of completeness," May 24, 2001 www.csmonitor.com/2001/0524/p23s1.html
"Whateverwhichway," April 23, 2001 www.csmonitor.com/2001/0423/p19s1.html
"One of 150," April 6, 2001 www.csmonitor.com/2001/0406/p23s1.html
"Crossroads," March 15, 2001 www.csmonitor.com/2001/0315/p19s1.html
"What the tide brings you," February, 28, 2001 www.csmonitor.com/2001/0228/p23s1.html
"The same to all observers," February 2, 2001 www.csmonitor.com/2001/0202/p23s1.html
"Not so fast," January 18, 2001 www.csmonitor.com/2001/0118/p23s1.html
"Ark building," December 29, 2000 www.csmonitor.com/2000/1229/p23s1.html
"Star stuff," December 22, 2000 www.csmonitor.com/2000/1222/p15s1.html
"What a view!" December 4, 2000 www.csmonitor.com/2000/1204/p23s1.html
"Magnificent buildings," November 30, 2000 www.csmonitor.com/2000/1130/p23s1.html
"'Go see Mike,'" November 16, 2000 www.csmonitor.com/2000/1116/p23s1.html
"Big moon and other illusions," November 10, 2001 www.csmonitor.com/2000/1110/p23s1.html
"Like gold," October 30, 2000 www.csmonitor.com/2000/1030/p19s4.html
"Attractive distractions," October 27, 2000 www.csmonitor.com/2000/1027/p23s1.html
"Oh, deer," September 28, 2000 www.csmonitor.com/2000/0928/p23s1.html
"Watch out, Denny's," September 12, 2000 www.csmonitor.com/2000/0912/p19s1.html
"Where's the number 4?" September 8, 2000 www.csmonitor.com/2000/0908/p23s1.html
"Always daytime," August 18, 2000 www.csmonitor.com/2000/0818/p23s1.html
"WAY better than tigers," August 8, 2000 www.csmonitor.com/2000/0808/p19s1.html
"Ozzulers and other things," August 7, 2000 www.csmonitor.com/2000/0807/p23s1.html
"Success story," August 1, 2000 www.csmonitor.com/2000/0801/p19s1.html
"On the run," July 13, 2000 www.csmonitor.com/2000/0713/p23s1.html
"An inspiring word," June 6, 2000 www.csmonitor.com/2000/0606/p19s1.html
"'Nothing's missing,'" May 18, 2000 www.csmonitor.com/2000/0518/p19s1.html
"Knowing what to look for," May 5, 2000 www.csmonitor.com/2000/0505/p23s1.html
"Life's moves," April 28, 2000 www.csmonitor.com/2000/0428/p23s1.html
"We are not powerless," April 21, 2000 www.csmonitor.com/2000/0421/p23s1.html
"The conviction that all is well," April 7, 2000 www.csmonitor.com/2000/0407/p23s1.html
"Seven promises and counting," March 28, 2000 www.csmonitor.com/2000/0328/p23s1.html
"The choice," February 14, 2000 www.csmonitor.com/2000/0214/p23s1.html
"Why we're here," January 14, 2000 www.csmonitor.com/2000/0114/p23s1.html
"In the details," October 1, 1999 www.csmonitor.com/1999/1001/p23s1.html
"Sermons in crosswords," March 19, 1999 www.csmonitor.com/1999/0319/p23s1.html
"The safety zone," April 27, 1998 www.csmonitor.com/1998/0427/042798.home.relarticle.1.html
"Tuning in to God," January 9, 1998 www.csmonitor.com/1998/0109/010998.home.relarticle.1.html

Christian Science Publishing Society—Pamphlets and CDs

Healing, "True Identity: A Conversation with Victor Westberg—Interview by Jeffrey Hildner,"
    pp. 11-20, 2007. (Pamphlet and CD).
Time, Space, Healing, "Conversation with Geoffrey Barratt—Interview by Jeffrey Hildner,"
    pp. 12-19, 2007. (Pamphlet and CD).
Parenting AZ, "The Choice," taped December 15, 2000 (CD: Special Collection series).

RECOMMENDED BOOKS: "Know Thyself"—and Know Others.
Books help us learn, change, and grow. You might get a lift out of some of the books that help me. I learned about most of them from other people. Each book hit me at just the right moment. I felt as if somebody handed me a gold coin.

You don't want to read these books unless you can handle the truth. They will turn your world inside out then right side up and never let you go. They teach you how life works and how to live in sync with principles as old as remembered time. In one way or another, these books speak to our heart's desire for wisdom, peace, and bliss.

I hope these authors, Spirit-gifted oracles, will do for you what they do for me and brave you forward on your quest.

Science and Health with Key to the Scriptures by Mary Baker Eddy
The Hero With A Thousand Faces by Joseph Campbell
The Message: The New Testament, Psalms and Proverbs by Eugene H. Peterson
The Writer's Journey by Christopher Vogler
The War of Art by Steven Pressfield
Story by Robert McKee
The Way of the Peaceful Warrior and other books by Dan Millman
The Tao of Daily Life by Derek Lin
The Last Word on Power by Tracy Goss
The One Thing You Need To Know and other books by Marcus Buckingham
Whatever You Think, Think the Opposite and other books by Paul Arden
Lateral Thinking and *Six Thinking Hats* by Edward de Bono
Language in Thought and Action by S.I. Hayakawa
Orbiting the Giant Hairball by Gordon MacKenzie
Illusions and *Jonathan Livingston Seagull* by Richard Bach
The Total Money Makeover by Dave Ramsey
The World Peace Diet by Will Tuttle
The Soul of Sex by Thomas Moore
Loving What Is by Byron Katie
The Power of TED* by David Emerald
Pay Attention, for Goodness' Sake by Sylvia Boorstein
The Way of the Superior Man by David Deida
Too Good to Leave, Too Bad to Stay and other books by Mira Kirshenbaum
The 5 Love Languages by Gary Chapman
Gifts Differing by Isabel Briggs Myers
The Strangest Secret by Earl Nightingale

Σ

Listen.

Wait.

∫

Don't move until you hear . . .

"And all these blessings shall come on thee, and overtake thee, if thou shalt hearken unto the voice of the Lord thy God." | Deuteronomy 28:2

All my life, I've seen Mind's startling power to rescue me from trouble and redesign my human experience in ways that leave me slack-jawed.

Help comes in all kinds of ways and not a beat too late: waves of calm and composure washed by the moonlight of clarity or by a steady beam from the lighthouse of hope . . . favorable configuration of circumstances behind the curtain . . . an invite out of the blue . . . a bus ride to serendipity.

I get signs all the time reassuring me that the divine Screenwriter loves my life-story and shapes it with mercy, music, and magic, including pressure-packed character tests, thunder-and-lightning scenes, and post-exile paradise like Chuck Noland in *Cast Away*.

My role? Listen. Listen to Mind, the divine Screenwriter. Listen to The Voice.

Like Josh Waitzkin in Steve Zaillian's moment-of-truth scene in *Searching for Bobby Fisher*, where Josh hears the voice of his chess coach silently urge, "Don't move until you see it," when it comes to the chess game of my life, I hear Coach urging me, "Don't move until you see it." And I don't. No matter how long it takes, I don't move until I hear The Voice.

Listen to The Voice

Don't move until you hear Me.
I can't hear you.
Don't move until you hear Me.
I can't hear you.
Don't move until you hear Me.

HOME.

"I will always be safe from the random hurricanes of outcome as long as I never forget where I rightfully live.

"I don't know where you rightfully live, but I know there's something in this world that you love more than you love yourself. Something worthy . . .

"You gotta identify the best, worthiest thing that you love most and then build your house right on top of it and don't budge from it.

"And if you should someday somehow get vaulted out of your home by either great failure or great success then your job is to fight your way back to that home the only way that it has ever been done, by putting your head down and performing with diligence and devotion and respect and reverence whatever the task is that love is calling forth from you next."

—Elizabeth Gilbert, TED Talk, "Success, failure and the drive to keep creating"

I KNOW WHERE I RIGHTFULLY LIVE:
IN THE **HOUSE OF THE METAPHYSICAL WARRIOR**.

MY ONE-WORD LIFE THEME: ARCHITECTURE.
Literally and figuratively.
The architecture of things visible.
And invisible.

The architecture of buildings,
paintings,
form and space,
as well as the architecture
of the inner and outer worlds of human life,
of archetypal patterns and emotional illusions,
and of the deep reality of Spirit.

MY ONE-WORD LIFE ANTHEM: TRUTH.
What is *really* going on?
Grasp the Truth,
and expect proof
to filter through and shape the architecture
of every dimension and detail
of your human life.

What is your One-Word Life Theme? *
What is your One-Word Life Anthem?

Hear The Voice assuring you:
**Now therefore my son,
the Lord shall be with thee,
and thou shalt prosper,
and *thou shalt build an house* to the Lord thy God,
as he hath spoken of thee.**
—1 Chronicles 22:11 (1599 Geneva Bible)

"I learned this, at least, by my experiment;

"The passage of the mythological hero may be overground, incidentally;

that if one advances confidently in the direction of his dreams,

fundamentally it is inward—into depths where obscure resistances

and endeavors to live the life which he has imagined,

are overcome, and long lost forgotten powers

he will meet with a success unexpected

are revivified, to be made available for the

in common hours."

transfiguration of the world."

—Henry David Thoreau

— Joseph Campbell,

The Hero with a Thousand Faces

*I thank my screenwriting teacher David McKenna for this concept (see *Memo from the Story Department*). Every character in a movie—and every adult in real life—lives according to their One-Word Life Theme, but 99% of us leave the planet never knowing our OWLT, because nobody ever told us that we have one. Figuring out mine (finally grasping the obvious!) changed my life and led me to discover the flip side of this Metaphysical Warrior Gold Coin: what I term our OWLA, *One-Word Life Anthem*. This Gold Coin, minted in the Treasury of Spirit, represents the currency of our identity. Thanks to Elizabeth Gilbert, I see that my One-Word Life Theme and One-Word Life Anthem represent where I rightfully live and what I love in this world more than I love myself, the foundation of my purpose and my heart—my character—on which I build my house and from which I will not budge.

"Know Thyself"—and Know Others.

Follow the thread of
the hero-path,
my friend.
Go forward with your
hero-heart
(wisdom, creativity,
empathy, and grit),
and listen to the hero-
voice of your divine
Spirit within.
Nothing can roadblock
your destination.
Mind's infinite power
shields you and your
special purpose from
confusion, mediocrity,
and lack.
Feel this infinite
Mind-power guarding
and guiding you—
rocketing you
to star-filled
galaxies of fulfillment
and bliss.

CONTROL AND SOUL

Rely on **META-CARE**: continuous Spirit-sourced well-being, including clarity, security, order, joy, health, and love.

ANTHEM

"In thee, O [MIND], do I put my trust; let me never be put to confusion."[1] I know what to do, and I know how to do it; I know what to say, and I know how to say it; I know if to do it and when to do it—because I coexist with and express MIND[2] as a sunbeam coexists with and expresses the sun.[3] What goes for me goes for everyone.

That's the truth. And I expect proof.

---

1 Psalms 71:1
2 "Immortal man was and is God's image or idea, even the infinite expression of infinite Mind, and immortal man is coexistent and coeternal with that Mind" (*Science and Health* by Mary Baker Eddy, p. 336).
3 "As a drop of water is one with the ocean, a ray of light one with the sun, even so God and man, Father and son, are one in being. The Scripture reads: 'For in Him we live, and move, and have our being'" (*Science and Health* by Mary Baker Eddy, p. 361).

"What is the key to wisdom?" anthropologist Carlos Castaneda asked an Argentinian wise man, who replied, "You must first find your place on the porch." JEF7REY HILDNER LIVES IN NORTHERN CALIFORNIA, where he spends porch-time in paradise . . . looking and listening.

An architect, a painter, and a writer, Hildner launched The Architect Painter Press in 2005 under the banner, "Live Brave." His award-winning work and his essays on the theory and practice of art appear in a wide range of publications, including *Journal of Architectural Education*, *Architectural Record*, and *Global Architecture Houses*. His project *Dante|Telescope House* won the New Jersey Chapter of The American Institute of Architects "Blue Ribbon Award for Excellence in Design."

Before leaving his full-time university career, he received the Association of Collegiate Schools of Architecture national award for excellence in teaching, and he continues to occasionally teach and lecture at schools of architecture.

Author of *Henry Trucks—Painter*, *Picasso Lessons*, *Garches 1234*, and *Daedalus 9*, as well as the noted essay "Formalism: Move | Meaning," featured in the book *Architectural Formalism*, Hildner has also written more than 225 articles on practical spirituality for *The Christian Science Monitor* and its sister magazines of The Christian Science Publishing Society, where he worked for nine years as a senior writer, a senior editor, and the creative director for *The Christian Science Journal* and *Christian Science Sentinel*.

As Hildner tries to safely navigate life's labyrinths and helps others to navigate their own, he continues to write, paint, and design buildings. He aims to conduct these endeavors and life in general as one grand Science-project, bringing the spirit of the Metaphysical Warrior, including "Expect Proof," to his daily adventure and long-term goals. The list of these goals includes a sequel to *Metaphysical Warrior*. Working title: *Metaphysical Warrior 2—Every Human Need*, a reference to the last three words of Mary Baker Eddy's line in *Science and Health*, "Divine Love always has met and always will meet every human need." In *Metaphysical Warrior 2*, Hildner will reveal more of his unique metaphysical insights and will report the results—flubs and fireworks!—of applying these insights to basic human needs, including money, food, friends, emotional intelligence, professional help, foresight, failure, trust, resilience, Coaching, character, and worthy ideals. The results in *Metaphysical Warrior 2* hinge on Hildner's ability to reach visions and dreams that currently lie beyond the horizon—where he hopes to soar, like Daedalus.

Hildner earned his undergraduate and graduate degrees from Princeton University.

Profile: www.thearchitectpainter.com/profile.html